WHY CAN'T
I
UNDERSTAND MY
KING JAMES BIBLE?

DR. BOBBY ADAMS, TH.D., PH.D.

Why Can't I Understand My King James Bible?

June, 2017

Copyright © 2017 by Dr. Bobby Adams

ISBN: 978-0-9987778-0-1

All Scripture quotes are from the King James Bible. Scripture quotes are in italics for emphasis.

Published by:
The Old Paths Publications, Inc.
142 Gold Flume Way
Cleveland, GA 30528
www.theoldpathspublications.com
TOP@theoldpathspublications.com

DEDICATION

This work is dedicated to my wife, Lea, who has unwaveringly stood with me for some 38 years now. She has unselfishly set aside her life and ministry in order to promote mine both in public and in our home.

I would also like to thank those quoted in this book who have unknowingly taught me the importance of the King James Bible. Also, were it not for the many hours and knowledge of computers of Dr. Kirk DiVietro, this book would never have been completed. Finally, James Stanley, who was my mentor for so many years, and taught me the love for the Bible, and how to study it.

Bobby J. Adams

TABLE OF CONTENTS

INTRODUCTION

You would think that of the over five million books in the world, that the Bible should be the easiest one to understand. After all, it is the word of God. And God gave it to mankind to reveal Himself to us. You would think that He would allow you to figure it out. Right?

You read your Bible like a good Christian. But something is amiss. You don't seem to receive as much from it as do other people. You have done what you were taught. You pray beforehand, asking God to reveal His word to you but nothing changes. You read the passage. You sit and stare at the words on the page and wonder, "What am I reading? What does it mean? What is going on in this chapter? Why am I still reading this Book?" Finally, in utter frustration, you close the Holy Scriptures and say, "There is no point in reading the King James Bible. No matter how hard I try I just cannot get anything out of it."

Is the Bible a closed book that only a select, elect group get to read with understanding and the rest are blinded to its truths and blessings? Did God set up His word in such a way that only the educated people can mine its treasures? Do the people who can translate the Scriptures into the English language from Hebrew, Aramaic, and Greek get to follow with ease the reading of the Bible while the rest of Christendom is left wondering when and if God will ever speak to them?

Or do you need some mystical key that only the "initiated" possess before its truths materialize? Does God give some mystery power to some and not others? Do the clergy have a spiritual leg up that lets them understand it?

That's the way many experience the Bible but is this the way that God intends it to be? If it is, then how will God hold those of us who do not understand, those of us who cannot understand the Bible accountable because we do not know what it says? That is not the God that the Bible describes. Either the Bible is an unsolvable mystery and God will not hold us accountable, OR, are there some clues that will help us to understand the Bible?

We believe that every child of God should be able to read the Bible and be touched by its truth. This book will attempt to explain why the Bible truth does not spontaneously jump from its pages to the hearts of people. It will attempt to aid its readers in hearing, obeying and enjoying things God has placed in the Bible for them.

Do the above words describe you? If they do, rest assured that you are not alone with your feelings. Did you know that before He went to the cross the Lord had already told His disciples everything that the Father had given Him to reveal? Yet they still did not understand His words. They even forgot some of them?

In John 15:15 Jesus said these words,

*All things that I have heard of my Father I
have made known unto you.*

His promise to the disciples is a promise to
you and me.

This should give us hope that God has done the
same for us in our King James Bible (KJB).

The Bible is the perfectly preserved word of
God without any proven errors. It is therefore, THE
Book that is alive and can mature you as a child of
God. It is His word that will save you, sanctify you,
and preserve you in this world. It will give you an
inheritance in the kingdom of God to come. What a
treasure that He has given us! But it will be an unused
hidden treasure unless we read, and live by it on a
daily basis for the rest of our lives!

Education, though at times can be a good
thing, will not help you or better equip you in
understanding God's word. You can know all the
vocabulary and grammar and still miss what God has
to say. A knowledge of original languages will not
help you to be a better student of the Scriptures. The
truth of God that feeds the spirit is found even in a
cold formal reading of the Scriptures.

Even if you were a Bible writer, who lived
when the Lord Jesus lived and taught, and could speak
Greek and Hebrew, you still would not necessarily be
guaranteed understanding of its pages. Peter said that
some of the things that Paul wrote were *"hard to be
understood."* Wise old Christians used to say, "The

best commentary on the Bible is the Bible. We will find the answer to our quandary in the Bible."

Our final authority in all matters pertaining to this book shall ever be the King James Bible. Our goal will be to understand what HE meant by what He wrote and how to apply it. To understand the Bible, it is of primary importance to know its Author. Then be humble, pray, run your references, and wait upon Him for truth.

Studying the Bible is like neurosurgery. When you have a medical condition, it is often good to have a second opinion. When you are dealing with neurology the more doctors you consult the more confused you will become. You find a doctor you trust and listen to him. Understanding the Bible is similar. The more versions you consult the more confused you will become. Another version cannot shed any light on God's true word, the perfectly preserved King James Bible.

This book will not give the person justification for laziness. The Bible tells us to seek out the word, read it, study it, meditate and memorize it, and then live by it. The Scriptures give us examples of those who have successfully complied with the above guidelines.

It is the author's purpose to list hindrances to understanding the Bible, and then give helps and guidelines to doing so. It will not be critiquing or correcting the Scriptures in the name of helping to make it reader friendly. The Bible must be respected and revered as Holy and separate from all other literary works known to man. No other book stands on the same level. Before this book is completed, it will contain helpful hints for those interested parties.

> [30] *And Philip ran thither to him, and heard him read the prophet Esaias, and said, Understandest thou what thou readest?* [31] *And he said, How can I, except some man should guide me? And he desired Philip that he would come up and sit with him.* Acts 8:30-31

> [20] *But ye have an unction from the Holy One, and ye know all things.* [27] *But the anointing which ye have received of him abideth in you, and ye need not that any man teach you: but as the same anointing teacheth you of all things, and is truth, and is no lie, and even as it hath taught you, ye shall abide in him.* 1 John 2:20, 27

Though this verse is speaking of the anointing which teaches us to abide in Christ, it is what it partially addressed herein. It is true that we need one another, but the main Teacher is the divine author of Holy Scripture, God the Holy Ghost.

Bobby Adams Th.D., Ph.D.
December 2014

BIBLICAL EXAMPLES

Biblical Examples

The Saviour Speaks

The first key to understanding the Bible is to read it and hear the voice of the Master Teacher, the Lord Jesus Christ Himself. He told us WHY we don't understand it. Let us list a few passages which shed some light on why you do not automatically understand the Bible.

In John 10:6 we read,

This parable spake Jesus unto them: BUT THEY UNDERSTOOD NOT WHAT THINGS THEY WERE WHICH HE SPAKE UNTO THEM.

The people who heard Jesus tell the parable spoke the same languages he spoke. They spoke Hebrew, Aramaic, and/or Greek so why did they not understand Jesus?

It wasn't just the general crowd that did not understand Jesus. Note that when the Lord was doing the teaching, his intimate disciples, the early church, often did not understand what He was talking about. We have proof of this phenomena in Matthew 15:15-17:

Then answered Peter and said unto him, Declare unto us this parable. And Jesus said, ARE YE ALSO YET WITHOUT UNDERSTANDING? DO NOT YE YET UNDERSTAND,....

Scriptures Hidden

Why didn't they understand what He was saying to them? The first thing that the Bible tells us is that some truths were purposely hidden. Certain truths were withheld until the listener was repentant and willing to obey them. Others were hidden because the hearers' ears were blocked by their sin.

Luke 9:45

But THEY UNDERSTOOD NOT this saying, AND IT WAS HID FROM THEM, that THEY PERCEIVED IT NOT: and they feared to ask him of that saying.

John 12:16

THESE THINGS UNDERSTOOD NOT HIS DISCIPLES at the first: but when Jesus was glorified, then remembered they that these things were written of him, and that they had done these things unto him.

Some passages are time sensitive. They may not be understood at the present time but perhaps later they become clear. We follow this principle in school. We do not teach students how to multiply until they can add. We do not tell students how to use grammar until they understand the parts of speech. In the same way, there are spiritual truths that we more easily understand when we have grown in the Lord and become a little more perceptive.

This principle also answers those who say that if they had been present when the Lord Jesus taught

God's words that they would understand the Scriptures better. The Bible says otherwise on several occasions as we are presently showing. In Matthew 13:10 the disciples came to Jesus and asked Him, *"Why speakest thou unto them in parables?"* Good question; for many still read the pages of Holy Writ and cannot understand the parables either.

Speaks In Parables

The Lord gave the answer in the next verse,

Because it is given UNTO YOU to know the mysteries of the kingdom of heaven, BUT UNTO THEM IT IS NOT GIVEN.
(v.11, emphasis mine)

It seems like Jesus often spoke to a targeted audience. If you are not part of that targeted audience you will not understand what he says.

Here the Lord gives a very interesting answer as to why He not only Speaks in parables but says that "it is not" for them to understand what He was saying. In Mark 4:33-34 we learn further,

And with many such parables SPAKE HE THE WORD unto them, AS THEY WERE ABLE TO HEAR IT.

The Lord spoke The Word to them and yet it was in parables, hidden from them, the crowd of people.

The text reminds us that He spoke AS THEY WERE ABLE TO HEAR IT. There are times that we are not able to hear the word of God whether reading or listening to it. Troubles, or other events of life often dull our spiritual ears. When that happens, we are not able to hear from God.

As a side note perhaps you would do well to ponder further Mark 4:11-12,

> *And he said unto them, Unto you it is given to know the mystery of the kingdom of God: but unto them that are without, all these things are done in parables: That seeing they may see, and not perceive; and hearing they may hear, and not understand; lest at any time they should be converted, and their sins should be forgiven them.*

Here is another thought to ponder taking the text just as it is. Parables are given so that they will not see, perceive, hear, understand and be converted, and their sins forgiven. This passage will be left up to the reader to figure out depending on your own theological persuasion.

Saved Person

Matthew discussed the same event. Matthew 13:19 adds an interesting point.

> *When any one heareth the word of the kingdom, and understandeth it not, then cometh the wicked one, and catcheth away that which was sown in his heart. This is he which received seed by the way side.*

The Lord Jesus is saying if you hear the word

and do not understand it, the wicked one catches or steals that word. Any word of God that you resist can be stolen by the Devil. The most important word God speaks is the word of Salvation. Jesus was not just a good teacher and perfect model for our lives. He came to give salvation. If you have heard the Gospel and not received it, Satan will steal the word of God to keep you from being saved.

One needs to be a saved person in order to understand God's word. The Scriptures are not black words on white pages. They contain the very breath of God. For them to be understood our human spirit must be alive. The Author of Scripture has to indwell you for you to get what God wants you to have from His word. This happens when you hear the word of God and believe it.

Add to this the previous text, Mark 4:11-12. This writer would say that if you see but do not perceive, hear but do not understand, then the devil has taken the word to keep you from being converted and having your sins forgiven. Strange thing about not understanding God's word, it's a dangerous thing too. Salvation may depend on obeying the Scriptures, but how can you if you do not understand it.

Stealing the Word

Luke 8:12, it puts it this way,

Those by the way side are they that hear; receive the with joy; then cometh the devil, and taketh away the word out of their

*hearts, LEST THEY SHOULD BELIEVE
AND BE SAVED.*

It just cannot get any plainer than that, friend.

When you go through the rest of these parables just listed you can see the importance of the seed, which is the word of God. That word can be *"choked with cares and riches and pleasures of this life, and bring no fruit to perfection"* as verse 14 says. Other things in this life can stop the word of God from becoming fruitful in our lives if we're not careful. You may not understand the Bible because it has been stolen from you by the evil one, cares of this life, or pleasures here in our life or in others. Riches cause many to stumble. Perhaps Asaph in Psalm 73:3 may not be the only one who stumbles in trusting God to take care of them when the wicked prosper instead of the righteous?

Secret Things

Has it ever occurred to you that perhaps some passages in Scripture are not for you to understand? The Bible says in Deuteronomy 29:29:

> *The secret things belong unto the LORD our God: but those things which are revealed belong unto us and to our children for ever, that we may do all the words of this law.*

In other words, there just might be some things in the Bible that are not for us to understand because they are hidden from us. All of us! Things, at times, do not make any sense to us. For example, when Jesus rose from the dead and appeared to the disciples on the road to Emmaus in Luke 24 and we read in verse 16, *"But their eyes were holden that they should not know him."* This was certainly deliberate on Jesus' part until He was ready to reveal Himself after opening their eyes. Then when He revealed Himself to them, Jesus vanished from their sight, literally. The Lord deliberately withheld Himself from them. Even so it is in many parables which are given in these parallel passages: Mtt. 13, Mk. 4, and Lk. 8 respectively.

Concerning parables, this author believes, that a parable is an exact, correct, infallible, and perfect teaching of a "doctrine" given in a veiled and mysterious form for a purpose. In Mark 4:2,

> And *HE TAUGHT THEM MANY THINGS BY PARABLES, and said unto them IN HIS DOCTRINE,...*

Once it is known that a parable teaches doctrine in a veiled form, the student of the word can figure out what Jesus is trying to convey to His listeners. Note too that if you do not like doctrine for whatever reason, then you would not have liked listening to the Lord Jesus, for He taught doctrine, He taught with authority.

Scriptures Fulfilled

In Matthew 13 again, in verse 14 we have an interesting thought. Scripture was fulfilled in them.

And in them is fulfilled the prophecy of Esaias, which saith, By hearing ye shall hear, and shall not understand; and seeing ye shall see, and shall not perceive:

Do you fall into that category? Since these were spoken of Jewish people of our Lord's day and their hearts were bad, and they were dull of hearing, and their eyes were closed to the things of God, it fulfilled Scripture in Isaiah 6:9-10,

And he said, Go, and tell this people, Hear ye indeed, but understand not; and see ye indeed, but perceive not. Make the heart of this people fat, and make their ears heavy, and shut their eyes; lest they see with their eyes, and hear with their ears, and understand with their heart, and convert, and be healed.

See also Jn. 12:37-41 where the Lord quoted from it.

Scriptures Opened

We need to have our spiritual eyes opened or we never will understand how to be saved, much less how to understand the Scriptures. The Scriptures have to be opened to us. In Matthew 16, when Jesus asked His disciples what people were saying about Him, Peter, in verse 16 says,

Thou art the Christ, the Son of the living God.

His response to Peter's Great Confession was,

Blessed art thou, Simon Bar-jona: for flesh

21

and blood hath not revealed it unto thee,
but my Father which is in heaven. (v. 17).

Now there's a wild idea! We cannot understand the Bible unless God Himself opens our minds and heart to see. This is the only way to see who Jesus really is and what He is saying to us. Unless God reveals Himself and His words to us we will never know who He is.

In Psalms 119:18, the Psalmist prayed,

Open thou mine eyes, that I may behold
wondrous things out of thy law.

In Acts 16:14, there was a lady named Lydia who *"worshipped God"* and listened to Paul, *"whose heart the Lord opened,...."* Understanding the Scriptures is a miracle of God. The Scriptures have to be opened to us. And through the Scriptures it has to be revealed that Jesus is the Saviour.

Our hearts, spiritually speaking, do have to be opened to receive the things freely given to us by God. They are not deduced by flawed human logic. In Luke 24:27, 31-32, we read:

> *And beginning at Moses and all the prophets, he expounded unto them in all the Scriptures the things concerning himself. And THEIR EYES WERE OPENED, AND THEY KNEW HIM; and he vanished out of their sight. And they said one to another, Did not our heart burn within us, while he talked with us by the way, and while HE OPENED TO US THE SCRIPTURES? (Emphasis is mine.)*

The Lord has to open and expound His word to us. The Spirit of God takes the things of Christ and shows them unto us Jn. 16:13-15. God's word is spiritually understood. His Holy Spirit takes the words perceived by our ears and eyes and causes our hearts to understand them. For in Jn. 16:15, we read,

> *All things that the Father hath are mine: therefore said I, that he shall take of mine, and shall shew it unto you.*

God has to show things unto us if we're to understand His words.

Spiritually Discerned

But why is this you might ask? We are told in 1 Corinthians 2:14,

> *But the natural man receiveth not the things of the Spirit of God: because they are spiritually discerned.*

The things of God have to be Spiritually "discerned" (Gen. 31:32, "knew"-known). If you do not know the Lord as your Saviour, then how can you know His words? The answer is that you cannot know, for they must be discerned.

The author of Scripture must live within us to make the things of God known to us say the two previous verses, 1 Corinthians 2:12-13. There are no other works known to man quite like the Bible. You see, you must know the Author of the Scriptures in order to understand His words. So, you must ask yourself, "Do you know the Lord as your Saviour?"

23

You must be Saved in order to understand God's word. Believe from the heart 1 Corinthians 15:3-4,

> *...[H]ow that Christ died for our sins according to the Scriptures; And that he was buried, and that he rose again the third day according to the Scriptures;*

and Romans 10:8-14 where we read in vs 9,

> *That if thou shalt confess with thy mouth the Lord Jesus, and shalt believe in thine heart that God hath raised him from the dead, thou shalt be saved.*

Study And Search The Bible

Even so, as believers this must be kept in mind. These are God's words and He must give the understanding. But we have a part in this process to *"rightly dividing the word of truth"* (2 Tim. 2:15). We must "Study" and "Search" (Jn. 5:39) the Scriptures. We must obey Acts 17:11 which says,

> *These were more noble than those in Thessalonica, in that they received the word with all readiness of mind, and SEARCH THE SCRIPTURES DAILY, whether those things were so.*

Prayer is vital in learning God's word along with studying it tirelessly. Ecclesiastes 12:12 reminds us,

> *And further, by these, my son, be admonished: of making many books there is no end; and much STUDY is a weariness of the flesh. (Emphasis is mine.)*

Have you studied to the point where you were worn out trying to understand God's word? Or you did not understand it, so maybe you re-read it and then kept on reading while raising an eye brow and let it go? Do you really want to get more out of reading your Bible, or are you a mere curiosity seeker thinking that it would be nice to understand it if possible, but said, "I'm not going to too much trouble"?

But, herein lies another reason *Why Can't I Understand My King James Bible?* The Bible has to be studied. Paul tells us in 2 Timothy 2:15,

Study to shew thyself approved unto God, a workman that needeth not to be ashamed, rightly dividing the word of truth.

The King James Bible has to be studied in order to "rightly" divide it. A cursory glance, or an over-view of the Scriptures simply is not adequate to be approved of by the Lord. Unless you study so as to be approved of by God Himself, you will be ashamed, for it will not be divided properly, much less be understandable. Studying in order to rightly divide it will take some time and effort on your part. Hence, dear reader, you simply must spend time in God's word if you are to understand its content.

Speaking Original Languages

Now, this brings us to yet another thought. Not only are there some parts of the Bible that would not be properly understood even if they were taught by

Christ, but now notice, if you possess an understanding of the original languages it will not necessarily help you either. Will you better understand the Bible if your capable of speaking its original languages?

The Apostle Peter wrote of Paul's writings, and though he had been with the Lord Jesus Himself, and was fluent in Greek and Hebrew, wrote that at least some of his writings were *"hard to be understood."* Listen to these words in 2 Peter 3:15-16,

> *...[E]ven as our beloved brother Paul also according to the wisdom given unto him hath written unto you; As also in all his epistles, SPEAKING in them of these things; IN WHICH ARE SOME THINGS HARD TO BE UNDERSTOOD, ...*

Let the reader be reminded that the Apostle Peter not only knew the biblical languages but also walked and talked with the Lord Jesus Christ Himself and heard His teaching. Yet he says that even for him some of Paul's writings were hard to understand. There are some things *"hard to be understood"* in Paul's epistles concerning the *"longsuffering of our Lord"* and future events, but not impossible. See 2 Thess. 2:1-5 (et al).

Much to the chagrin of our scholarly brethren, language studies do not always yield the answers that we sometime seek. More often than not, humility of mind, patience of time, seeking the Lord, and searching the Scriptures yield understanding more than mere language studies. While waiting on the Lord, you might need to keep reading and searching the Bible before giving up. So, work through the Bible while you are waiting on the Lord to give you understanding.

Spoke Under Inspiration

In 2 Timothy 3:16 we read,

All SCRIPTURE IS GIVEN BY INSPIRATION OF GOD, and is profitable for doctrine, for reproof, for correction, for instruction in righteous:...

Again, in 2 Peter 1:21 we read,

For the prophecy came not in old time by the will of man: but holy men of God spake as they were moved by the Holy Ghost.

Another thing that many think is that if they were a prophet who spoke under inspiration or were a Bible writer using biblical languages that they would better understand the Holy Scriptures. Again may we look to see "what saith the Scriptures" about this matter. In 1 Peter 1:10-12,

Of which salvation (of your souls[1] v.9) the prophets have enquired and searched diligently, who prophesied of the grace that should come unto you; Searching what, or what manner of time the Spirit of

---

[1] 1 Peter 1:9 Receiving the end of your faith, even the salvation of your souls

Christ which was in them did signify, when it testified beforehand the sufferings of Christ, and the glory that should follow. Unto whom it was revealed, that not unto themselves, but unto us they did minister the things, which are now reported unto you by them that have preached the gospel unto you with the Holy Ghost sent down from heaven; which things the angels desire to look into.

Imagine that. That the prophets made diligent enquiry of the things that they were inspired to write but did not understand the sufferings and the glory of Christ–these were Holy Scriptures they were searching which they had penned down. This is absolutely mind-boggling to consider, dear reader.

A prophet of God can write under inspiration and not understand what he is writing even after making diligent search for understanding. If you, the reader, should like to see an example of a Bible writer who did not understand what he saw in a vision, then go and read the following verses: Dan. 7:15-16, 19, 28; 8:15-19, 27; 10:7-12, 14, 21; 12:4, 8-9. Then, too recall that Daniel penned the words of the angelic messenger down and it is Scripture. These verses in Daniel deal primarily with Israel during the end times. Maybe now you have some idea of what Peter wrote, which is quoted above.

So, in order to understand the Bible, you must be saved and have the Spirit, Who is the Author, to indwell you. However, there are secret things that belong unto the Lord contained in the Bible. Also, there are Scriptures to be fulfilled and have to be opened to us, spiritually discerned, and then studied.

So, yes, at first reading the Bible does seems a formidable task to the novice. But keep on reading, re-reading, searching, studying, running those cross references, be in prayer, trust the Lord to show you His words, talk to spiritually-minded believers and your pastor as well. But meditate on the word of God for as long as you can while in prayer before taking the easy way out.

At this point it may not be wise to check a commentary, lexicon, or a dictionary. Those are always a last resort. Develop a 'do it yourself attitude' before calling for help. Allow God to speak to you through His word, opening it up to you. In Proverbs 6:22 we read,

> *When thou goest, it shall lead thee; when thou sleepest, it shall keep thee; and when thou awakest, it shall talk with thee.*

Imagine, the word of God speaking to you, leading you, and giving you instruction. Wow, that's a wild concept, the 'talking Bible'? Now go a step farther and imagine that as you read the Bible you are actually hearing God speak. Don't read the Bible as an essay on theology. HEAR God speaking to you personally through His perfectly preserved KJB.

Remember, that Job 32:8 says that the inspiration of God Almighty gives us understanding of His words, so, be encouraged as you study the book.

Sound Doctrine

Turning attention to Matthew 22:23-33 there a case of, at the very least, a situation where sound doctrine comes up, which can hinder one's ability to understand the Scriptures. From verse 23 the reader is introduced to a group of religious people called *"the Sadducees, which say that there is no resurrection,"* They asked the *"Master"* (v. 24) meaning Christ, a hypothetical situation, though you can see it in Genesis 38:9-10; Deut. 25:9; Ruth 4:5, 8, 16 in an effort to trap Him in His speech from the Law. But from verse 29 Jesus told them that they *"do err, not knowing the Scriptures, nor the power of God."*

Jesus told them that there will be no marriage between people in heaven but instead they will be like the angels who do not marry (they are all males biblically speaking).

Further, the Sadducees did not believe in angels either (Matt. 3:7), Jesus was exposing another of their false beliefs. According to one writer, Jesus' argument was built on the emphatic present tense "I AM" in Exo. 3:6 and it silenced the Sadducees (v. 34). Sometimes if one has unsound exegesis of Scripture it prohibits their understanding of the Scripture. It is very important to have sound doctrine or biblical principles in place when interpreting the Bible. But if you have a false view such as these

Sadducees, it prevents you from understanding the Bible. Over and over the Apostle Paul exhorts Timothy and Titus in his pastoral epistles to be sure to have "sound doctrine" or "wholesome words" or "sound speech" (1 Tim. 1:10; 4:16; 5:17; 6:1;   2 Tim. 1:13; 2:15; 3:10, 16; 4:2-3; Titus 1:9; 2:1, 5, 7-8, 10, plus phrases like "the truth" 1 Tim. 2:4; 3:15; 4:3; 6:5; 2 Tim. 2:15, 18, 25; 3:7-8; 4:4; Titus 1:1, 14). Try to explain some passages to those who are not sound in some areas in the Bible and they cannot understand what you're talking about. Allow the Bible to give you your doctrine. Don't bring doctrine to the Bible and force it to fit your preconceived ideas.

Severity

Now consider Mark 8:17, 21,

And when Jesus knew it, he saith unto them, Why reason ye, because ye have no bread? Perceive ye not yet, neither understand? HAVE YE YOUR HEART YET HARDENED?... How is it that ye do not understand?

Friend, could it be possible that another reason that you find the Bible to be hard to follow, is because of Severity, that is, you have a hardness about you? "Maybe there is sin in our lives, and we cannot hear the words of the Bible. We are aware of the fact that if there is sin in our lives that our prayers can be hindered (Isaiah 59:2), but what about in reading God's word?"

A case in point is Matthew 19, where the Pharisees were trying to tempt Jesus, asking Him in verse 3 about it being lawful or right for a man to divorce his wife for any reason. Then in verse 8, Jesus uses our current phrase, "hardness of heart",

> *Moses because of the HARDNESS OF YOUR HEART suffered you to put away your wives: but from the beginning it was not so.*

Because of the hardness of their heart they thought it was okay to divorce their wives "for any reason", they did not understand what the Scriptures had to say on that subject. Could this be part of your problem? Having hardness of heart will prevent you from getting from God's word what you need to receive from it.

It is a good idea to always pray and not only ask God's guidance as we read His word, but also "confess our sins" (1 John 1:9) to Him. It has been said, "Reading the Bible will keep you from sin or sin will keep you from reading the Bible"[2], and this author completely agrees.

Now, there may yet be another thought on this matter of hardness of the heart as is found in Mark's account in 8:17-21. Here, after the feeding of the 4,000, the disciples forgot to take some bread to eat but the one loaf that was already on board the ship. Jesus told them to *"beware of the leaven of the*

---

[2] Paraphrased in English from Martin Luther

Pharisees, and of the leaven of Herod" in verse 15. To which, when the Lord knew it, He asked, in verse 17, "...*perceive ye not yet, neither understand? Have ye your heart yet hardened?"*

Then in the next verse Jesus said of them that you have eyes to see this miracle do you not? You have ears and have just heard Me speak have you not? So, what is there not to understand? (See, verses 18, 21). Another added thought here is a slight problem for many today in not understanding the Bible.

Have you ever thought about the fact that the reason that you understand some verses and not others is because you do not "remember" what you read? This may seem trite or silly but a forgetful hearer or a reader, why continue showing them anything, as they will not remember, much less take heed, to what is written? Why should God show you any more in the Bible when you're not obeying what you previously read?

You see friend, a forgetful person according to the text is one who is *"not a doer"* of the word. If you do not obey what you know to do, obey the Bible, then you are a forgetful hearer. James 4:17.

In James 1:22-25 we read,

But be ye doers of the word, and not hearers only, deceiving your own selves. For if any be a hearer of the word, AND NOT A DOER, he is like unto a man beholding his natural face in a glass: For he beholdeth himself, and goeth his way, and STRAIGHTWAY FORGETTETH what manner of man he was. But whoso looketh into the perfect law of liberty, and continueth therein, he being NOT A FORGETFUL HEARER, but a doer of the work, this man shall be blessed in his deed.

Ceremony

Now, let's go back a chapter to Mark 7 and consider verses 13, and 18. Has it occurred to you my friend that you can make the word of God of none effect in your lives by traditions? You see, the word of God works according to Acts 20:32; 1 Thess. 2:13; Heb. 4:12. For we are told that it's the word of God

"...which is able to build you up, and to give you an inheritance among all them which are sanctified."

For this the word of God which ye heard of us, ye received it not as the word of men, but as it is in truth, the word of God, WHICH EFFECTUALLY WORKETH ALSO IN YOU THAT BELIEVE.

For the word of God is quick, and powerful, and sharper than any two-edged sword, piercing even to the dividing asunder of soul and spirit, and of the joints and marrow, and is a discerner of the thoughts and intents of the heart.

So, having established the point of the word of God which works in us that believe, we may now consider Mark chapter 7. Remember our quest here is to understand why many have trouble understanding God's word, the King James Bible, because of traditions.

The Lord Jesus tells us in verse 13, that there are some people who are,

> *Making the word of God of NONE EFFECT THROUGH YOUR TRADITION, which ye have delivered: and many such like things do ye.*

Again, in verse 18 He asks,

> *"...Are ye so without understanding also?..."*

This can be called Ceremony which prevents one from seeing what God means in any given passage.

The context of v. 13 is an individual calling his possessions *"Corban"* or *"a gift"* verse 11, because a son is angry with his parents. This type of *"gift"* could only be used for service to God, thus they could not benefit financially (see Exo. 20:12; 21:17; Numbers 30:2). But this practice was condemned by the Lord Jesus by showing that the Pharisees and scribes were guilty of canceling out God's word to honor his parents through their own traditions. You see, then the Pharisees and the scribes would receive the benefits of the son's possessions. For instance, if you have a certain way that you do things and that is different than what is in the Bible, it causes you to not understand it. Why? Because you're seeking to justify your habit or tradition and if a passage goes against it you're confused with that verse.

So it is in this passage, the religious leaders wanted the son's possessions and figured out a way to get them by referring to those possessions as corban. By so doing then the parents couldn't have them but the religious crowd could. They voided out the Old Testament verses on the subject of possessions by making something up, a loophole, as it were, in order to get what they wanted.

In the next example given for the context of v. 18–since food is merely physical, no one who eats it will defile his heart which is spiritual. External ceremonies and rituals cannot cleanse a person spiritually. So, by overturning the ceremony of hand washing, Christ says that it removed the restrictions about dietary laws.

What a person says and does comes out of a defiled heart. Again, traditions void or cancel out the authority of God's word. Matthew 15:11 puts it this way,

> Not that which goeth into the mouth defileth a man; but that which cometh out of the mouth, this defileth a man.

When the heart is corrupt then the life and conduct will be corrupt. But if the heart is clean the life will be clean as well and the fruit will be good. The Lord is illustrating by the parable told here in Mk. 7:15 that nothing edible is defiling to the man.

However, please understand that Jesus was not talking about poisons, narcotics, intoxicating drinks, tobaccos and many other things that will destroy our bodies. Put in another way, the externals cannot cleanse a person spiritually or internally. So, there is a contrast here, between food and sins of the heart, which is the true source of either sin or righteousness.

Seeking Glory

In John 8 there seems to be another reason that people struggle with understanding the word of God, this is Self-Seeking Glory or self-serving. How can you decipher God's words if you are in fact seeking glory for your own self? Recall 1 Corinthians 1:29,

That no flesh should glory in his presence.

And again, 1 Cor. 1:31,

That, as it is written,[3] He that glorieth, let him glory in the Lord.

Now in John 8:27 there is again a case where the disciples did not understand the Lord, this time "They understood not that he spake to them of the Father." So Jesus told them in verse 28,

...When ye have lifted up the Son of man, then shall ye know that I am he, and that I do nothing of myself; but as my Father hath taught me, I speak these things.

To those the text says that believed on Him He

---

[3] Jeremiah 9:23-24

spoke of being made free if they continue in the truth. Jesus was not speaking to the religious leaders, but they replied anyway in verse 33,

> *...We be Abraham's seed, and were never in bondage to any man: how sayest thou, Ye shall be made free?*

Then Jesus began to explain in the next ensuing verses about being held as a captive to sin. He acknowledged them as being Abraham's seed, 8:37,

> *...but ye seek to kill me, because my word hath no place in you.*

But, they said that

> *...Abraham is our father*

and here in verse 39-40 the Lord reminds them that Abraham did not try to change the truth or try and kill one who hears from God.

After telling them they were not of Abraham's seed but rather of their father the devil, He said, in verse 42,

> *If God were your Father, ye would love me: for I proceeded forth and came from God; neither came I of myself, but he sent me.*

In verse 43 Jesus said,

> *Why do ye not understand my speech? even because ye cannot hear my word.*

Then Jesus told them that they are of their father the devil. Now the Lord had told them why that they could not understand His speech,

> And because I tell you the truth, ye believe
> me not (v. 45).

They were not of God so they could not hear His words because they were not of God according to verse 47. Then they replied that Jesus had a devil to which He said in verses 49-50a,

> ...I have not a devil; but I honour my
> Father, and ye do dishonor me. And I seek
> not mine own glory:....

They who were not of God, but of their father the devil, did not believe what Jesus was saying, and could not hear what He was saying because they were glorying in themselves by dishonoring Christ. By saying that He was not seeking His own glory Jesus was telling them that they were seeking their own glory.

In John 5:44 Jesus tells why that they could not believe.

> How can ye believe, which receive honour
> one of another, and seek not the honour
> that cometh from God only?

Are you having a hard time believing the word of God? Perhaps it's because you secretly want vain glory. Lucifer wanted that as the Scripture says, Isaiah 14:13-14; Ezekiel 28:12, 15, 17.

If you are seeking your own glory, your own agenda, trying to build yourself up on how much you've read in the Bible or how much you read the Bible or how much you know about the Bible, then you will not desire to read the Bible because you love the Lord.

You may read it in order to have bragging rights but not to honor the Lord and to grow in His word in order to draw closer to Him. You will not be interested in becoming more like the Lord, because you want to argue your point. You're all about having people think just how smart you are in Bible knowledge. You are in point of fact trying to impress people with your knowledge. Man naturally seeks to have honor among other men.

Would you like to see something about believing the Bible? Not believing the Bible is a tremendous reason why people do not understand it by the way. This goes along somewhat with this idea of believing what you are hearing the Bible say to you. In Mark 9:9-10 we read,

> *And as they came down from the mountain, he charged them that they should tell no man what things they had seen, till the Son of man were risen from the dead. And they kept that saying with themselves, questioning one with another what the rising from the dead should mean.*

Again, the disciples, the Lord's church, did not know exactly what He meant by that statement. Now, they were aware of what it meant on other occasions, so what is going on in this passage? Look in Mk. 8:31-32, where the Lord Jesus told them that He would *"suffer, and be killed, and after three days rise again"* that *"Peter took him, and began to rebuke him."* Then in the very next passage, verse 33, it says of Jesus,

> But when he had turned about and looked on his disciples, he rebuked Peter, saying, Get thee behind me, Satan: for thou savourest not the things that be of God, but the things that be of men.

Though Peter heard what the Lord just said about rising from the dead, he did not believe it, and rebuked Jesus for saying it. But, he did understand what He meant.

Again, in John 11 with nearly the whole chapter dealing with raising Lazarus from the dead, we read what his sisters understood about the resurrection of the dead. Look in verses 23-24, where we read,

> Jesus saith unto her, Thy brother shall rise again. Martha saith unto him, I know that he shall rise again in the resurrection at the last day

So, obviously, there is a problem of believing the sacred Scriptures going on in the text.

The author suspects that that is precisely why people do not understand the Bible better, they just do not believe it. Here, Martha believed that a resurrection would take place somewhere out in the future called *"the last day."* The Bible speaks more specifically as to when this will take place, according to 1 Thessalonians 4:13-18 and in Revelation 20:5-6 at the Rapture of the saints, called *"the first resurrection."*

Something Carried Now

For the next point, consider John 16:12,

I have yet many things to say unto you, but ye CANNOT BEAR THEM NOW. (Emphasis mine)

At this particular time, the disciples were not able to Carry Something Now. Why? The very next verse (13) tells us that the Holy Ghost would make known the other truths when the proper time came.

There are times in our lives that we just cannot understand certain truths at a given point. So, be patient, keep on reading the Bible through and through, and when the right time comes, God will show you what the text says. But just think about this point for a while; there are some things in the Bible that we may never understand. We're simply not ready to see the truth of a passage, or it is not God's will at the present time.

This word *"bear"* is used of the Lord in John 19:17, *"And he bearing his cross went forth."* The Lord used it when He denounced religious leaders in Luke 11:46.

Woe unto you also, ye lawyers! For ye lade men with burdens grievous to be borne, and ye yourselves touch not the burdens with one of your fingers.

This word "bear" means in the sense of carrying something. The withheld teaching from the Lord would be more than the disciples were able to carry at this point in their lives.

On a lighter note, it is good of the Lord not to lay on us more than we can bear or carry! This passage in John 16 should give us hope that as we grow in the Lord, that more verses will come to light.

Some Concluding Remarks

The above points are earnestly given as some possible reasons as to why many Bible readers receive little understanding of Scripture and have low comprehension of what they have just read. Someone who means a great deal to this writer once said, "I read the Bible through and couldn't understand it." So, the above thoughts or hindrances may be things that hold you back from being a happy regular Bible reader and or teacher.

But do not be discouraged, keep on reading the Scriptures! Apply the above suggestions to the seeming problems and grow in the Lord. The keys are to make sure that you know the Lord as your Saviour, pray and spend as much time as possible in the word. Try not to let things that you do not understand prevent you from reading. Remember, no one individual understands all of the Bible no matter how long they've been saved, no matter how many times that they've read it through, no matter how many versions of the Bible are available to him.

Run your references in your Bible to help your comprehension skills, and wait on the Lord.

Remember too, that the Bible is to be read time and time again, and it must be studied. There are a number of King James Bible readers whom God has taught that will gladly be of assistance if you will just ask them. Please do not use the above possible reasons as excuses to quit reading God's word. Stay in the word, attend a Bible-believing church and watch God work in your life to help you grow as a Christian.

BIBLICAL EXPRESSIONS

Biblical Expressions

Introduction

In January of 1604 King James I of England commissioned a translation of the Bible without all the notes of the Geneva Version. Though the "King was for appointing 54 learned men," the number "actually employed" was 47 Biblical Scholars by July of that same year. (Alexander McClure's, *The Translators Revived*, Mobile, AL, R. E. Publications, 1858, 1974. p. 66).

David Daniel, in *The Bible in English*, on page 438, tells his readers that Lancelot Andrewes, one of the directors of two companies at Westminster, mentions the work had been regularly scheduled in November of that same year of 1604. Adam Nicholson's book, *God's Secretaries* on page 154 relates that the Oxford Company didn't begin their work until February 13, 1605. It is this writer's understanding that the King James Bible was finished by late 1608 and each of the 6 groups reviewed the other groups work in 1609. Then it was reviewed by a 12-man committee for the next 9 months, sometime in 1610. Finally, two men examined it yet again totaling at least 14 times it had been gone over.

According to *"An Historical Account of The English Versions of The Scriptures,"* The English Hexapla, page 153, every part had been examined at least 14 times, 36 distinctly, "many parts fifteen times, and some seventeen."

The point being made here is, if the Bible has been gone over this many times, then the reader should be able, in time, to have confidence in and a better understanding of it. It was sent to the printer and it was published and came out on May 2, 1611 AD.

The Title page of my Bible reads:

THE HOLY BIBLE CONTAINING THE OLD AND NEW TESTAMENTS TRANSLATED OUT OF THE ORIGINAL TONGUES AND WITH THE FORMER TRANSLATIONS DILIGENTLY COMPARED AND REVISED BY HIS MAJESTY'S SPECIAL COMMAND.

The translational philosophy of the KJB translators was, I believe, to be a literal text, a linguistic text, and as literary a text as possible. This philosophy seems to me to be foreign to Bible societies of today. Their belief was to translate the Biblical languages as literal as possible. So, they adopted what's called the Verbal Equivalence or the Formal Translation Technique, according to Dr. D. A. Waite in his book, *Defending the King James Bible.* However, this is foreign or contrary to the modern way of translating which is called Dynamic Equivalence, which is little more than saying, "in other words." This method implies, as Waite continues, change and moving away from the literal word-for-word way of translating the Hebrew, Aramaic, and Greek words into English. Though there are many, I believe, examples of literally translating the Bible into English, I will give only two examples.

Literal Text

An example from Hebrew to English in the Old Testament would be Genesis 1:1,

> *"In the beginning God created the heaven and the earth."*

An example from Greek to English in the New Testament would be John 1:1,

> *"In the beginning was the Word, and the Word was with God, and the Word was God."*

The KJB is a Literal Translation. For some of you, this is a reason why you say that you cannot understand the KJB, because it is a literal translation. However, let's examine this literal translation method to see what it would mean to use some other translation of Scripture utilizing another method of translating. In other words, what kind of a Bible would you have if another method other than a literal one is used?

Well, for one thing, you would not have God's word now would you? If you read God's word in the Daniel Bomberg Hebrew Edition of 1524-1525, which is the Ben Chayyim Masoretic Text called the Second Rabbinic Bible, for the Old Testament, and in the Textus Receptus Beza's 5th edition of 1598 or Scrivener's Annotated Greek New Testament word for word only for it to be translated into English of the KJB using a concept theory, where the thoughts or main idea is given, how it would feel?

If only half of the text was translated into English, is it all of God's words? What do you do with the remaining words left in the text? Other questions might be: How many words should be left out of a text? Do you take out some Hebrew and Greek words enough to form a complete thought, or sentence?

But what if other thoughts can be conveyed with the rest of the other words left untranslated into English? What does the translator do in this situation? Then you only have part of what God originally said and that's according to the translators' opinions or style of translating, right? Right. Of course this is true, therefore, the literal method is the only course of action that you can take in translating Scripture. You want what God said, not what He meant, or thought, or is trying to convey, and that according to which translator you're reading after.

If, at the reading of the last will and testament of a deceased loved one, would you want read what they actually said, or only what they meant? Our Lord left instructions about Himself, His will, and His testaments, containing the past, present, and the future of our lives, other's lives, and the next life.

So, do you want only what He meant or what He said? As for this writer, what the Lord really said is what is wanted to be read. Besides, this is what the Scriptures tell us that God has accomplished in making His WORDS available to us. *"What saith the Scripture?"* In Matthew 4:4 we read,

> *But he answered and said, It is written, Man shall not live by bread alone, but by EVERY WORD THAT PROCEEDETH OUT OF THE MOUTH OF GOD.* (emphasis is to live, according to "every word", "that proceedeth out of the mouth of God."

If, according to some, that we are not sure if we have all that God said, we only have essentially what He said, then how can we obey this verse? If we do not have what God actually said, only what He meant, or the main ideas or concepts, how can we live our lives *"BY EVERY WORD"?*

If we do not have His every word He said, then we cannot live by it; they are missing. We are left to the whims of a translator, and he is our authority for what God said. So, now do you see the importance of living by word for word or a literal translation of what God said, as opposed to what the translator's opinions are? You want what God said, *"Thus saith the Lord."* Therefore, it is not what God said in the KJB that is your problem for not understanding it, for it is literally what He said. We are accustomed to this method all of the time are we not?

For instance: We send a messenger to give a message to another person, and when that messenger returns, we enquire what that person SAID, NOT WHAT DID HE MEAN. That is the point, right? Admittedly, you may ask what did he mean by that, since the messenger spoke with the person you sent a message to, but the main objective is what they said.

So, it is with the Holy Bible, we want what God actually said, and that we can be sure of, but only in the KJB. By the way, have you noticed these expressions in the KJB, as in the above cited reference, *"he answered and said"*? See that, that is literal, for it does not merely say, that He (Jesus) answered, but both "answered" and "said" are used. Modern versions don't understand this point.

Linguistic Text

Next, there are examples of translating Linguistically in the Scriptures. To be sure, the translators themselves were all linguists in their own right. A linguist is one who studies languages.

John Bois for instance began studying Hebrew at the age of 5 and by 6 years of age was writing it legibly.

Lancelot Andrews of the Westminster group in the Old Testament, and president at that, had acquired most of the languages of Europe. He could speak fluently some 15 total just as well as his native tongue, by trying to learn a language in a month. It was said that he did his private devotions in Greek, and had he been at the Tower of Babel he could have been their interpreter.

So, the list and their remarkable abilities are almost unsurpassed even by today's standards.

One linguistic example might be Luke 2:12, which started out saying, "take this for a signe" and "childe swadled, laid", and was changed to "this shall be a signe vnto you" and changed again to "babe wrapped in swaddling clothes laying in a manger" to finally reading in 1611, "And this shall be a signe vnto you, Ye shall finde the babe wrapped in swadling clothes laying in a manger." The word "laying" was changed to "lying" later on.

Now of course, since spelling has been standardized (by 1769), the letter e has been dropped and the letter v changed to the letter u, and an additional letter d is added to the word "swaddling."

Further, the words "shall be" are in italics because they were supplied by the translators to aid the reader. These were linguistic decisions made to this text and countless other examples could be cited to prove the point. This information comes from *Coming of the King James Gospels: A Collation of the Translators' Work-in-Progress*, by Ward S. Allen, and Edward C. Jacobs, page 7. The KJB is a Linguistic Translation.

Literary Text

Then too, the KJB is a Literary masterpiece of translation, and can be proved nearly anywhere you look in its pages. Perhaps John 3:16 is the best known, loved, and quoted example of Scripture being written in a literary style for reading purposes. The verse just flows in a masterful way for memorization purposes as well. This is what many love about the KJB even among its most outspoken and ardent critics.

For God so loved the world, that he gave his only begotten Son, that whosoever believeth in him should not perish, but have everlasting life.

It is interesting to note that, "Dictionaries and thesauruses of Greek words and phrases were examined for meaning and nuance, including the lexicon of obscure Greek words compiled by the fifth-century grammarian Hesychius of Alexandria" from *Manifold Greatness: The Making of the King James Bible*, Edited by Helen Moore and Julian Reid, p. 102.

The translators had Hebrew and Greek Bibles, grammars, dictionaries, commentaries, theological works, and sermons on difficult passages they referenced throughout their translational work on the Scriptures. They had access to Martin Luther's Bible written in the German language, and Italian works to list only two works.

But that's not all that they had, for these are all to be expected. Would it surprise the reader to learn that they also referenced books dealing with many differing types of insects and creatures in different languages, and rabbinical writings in Aramaic, and even classical literature written in different languages as well? Besides all these things, they were exceeding well-nigh experts of the English language.

With esteemed and well educated men in the English language such as Richard Mulcaster, Edmund Spenser and Thomas Kyd, these last two men "were at home with the genres of poetry and drama, in a way that we are no longer attuned to listening to sermons or analyzing the language and phrasing of biblical prose" (Moore and Reid, pp.81-82).

Punctuated Text

So, one of the many criticisms hurled against the KJB is its much-used punctuation marks throughout along with its grammar.

Are you kidding me? These men had command of the English tongue, lectured in Greek and Latin including their personal devotions, and became fellows at college by the age of 16. They were expected to translate from Latin to Greek with ease, to be able to converse and to debate in those languages as if they were their very own. They had to know the different types of literary genres, and to be attuned to harmony, cadence and rhythm for both the written as well as the spoken word. Moore and Reid continue on page 66 that there were some men who taught themselves three languages: Hebrew, Syriac, and Aramaic and went on to have official teaching positions.

Now, as to the allocation of too much punctuation, explanation will now be given. Leland Ryken in his book, *The Legacy of the King James Bible*, mentions on page 56 that the KJB is "too heavily punctuated" by todays' standards. But he adds that they had in mind that the Bible is "appointed to be read in churches." The punctuation is used to guide the public reading of Scripture, and how the people were to hear it read.

The Bible is rhythmic, that is, it "flows smoothly off the tongue and into the ear of the listener... (it, my word) gets registered by such words as dignity and eloquence." (Ryken, p. 61).

Saying that the Bible is too punctuated or has literary excellence are not points or marks against it, rather, it speaks highly in favor of the Bible.

To give only a few examples of punctuation and smooth eloquent sounding words, though one can look nearly anywhere, the passage in Ephesians chapter one will suffice. Consider verses 3-6, and it's all one sentence.

> *Blessed be the God and Father of our Lord Jesus Christ, who hath blessed us with all spiritual blessings in heavenly places in Christ: According as he hath chosen us in him before the foundation of the world, that we should be holy and without blame before him in love: Having predestined us unto the adoption of children by Jesus Christ to himself, according to the good pleasure of his will, To the praise of the glory of his grace, wherein he hath made us accepted in the beloved.*

My, my, now is that not beautiful? This is an example piece of an elegant literary masterful writing. Did you happen to notice the punctuation as well? The colons are given to cause you to pause and consider what is being said, and the commas are inserted to help you to know where to begin to give voice inflection. They aid you in the reading process.

Further, the truth, such as theology and doctrine being taught in these marvelous verses gives calm assurance of the mighty workings of God on our behalf because of Christ. Throughout this chapter are other examples of the same type of phenomena. See for example verses 7-12; this would take expositor's weeks to teach any congregation the truth of God's word. Again, this only strengthens the KJB or the AV as God's proven, providential, and perfectly pure, and preserved word of God in English.

Thomas Boys has well said (Commentary, 1 Pet. 3),

> There is much in the Holy Scriptures, which we find it hard to understand: nay, much that we seem to understand so fully as to imagine that we have discovered in it some difficulty or inconsistency. Yet the truth is that passages of this kind are often the very parts of the Bible in which the greatest instruction is to be found: and, more than this, the instruction is to be obtained in the contemplation of the very difficulties by which at first we are startled. This is the intention of these apparent inconsistencies. The expressions are used, in order that we may mark them, dwell upon them, and draw instruction out of them. Things are put

to us in a strange way, because, if they were put in a more ordinary way, we should not notice them.

Repetitions in the Text

Now, let's move onto Biblical Expressions that you may have some struggles with, for whatever reason, as you read the Bible. To begin with, let's deal with Repetition of words, phrases, and verses which seem redundant. In Exodus 35:22 for example, towards the end of the verse we read, "*and every man that offered offered an offering of gold unto the LORD.*" How is that for a tongue-tied or brain teasing, repetitious exercise, depending whether you read it aloud or not? Again, it says, "*offered offered an offering*" for by today's standards it is unacceptable huh? However, this is the way that in ancient Jewish culture the Hebrew speaking people loved to write their language, using repetition, parallel statements, and alliteration of letters or sounds.

Note: In the next division, the italicized words will be addressed. Consider the following examples of repetition found throughout the Bible.

Numbers 18:21, *"Their service which they serve."*

1 Samuel 7:10, *"Thundered with a great thunder."*

2 Samuel 1:17, *"Lamented with this lamentation."*

Psalms 13:3, *"Sleep the sleep."*

> Mark 5:42, *"And they were astonished with a great astonishment."*

Before going to the best example of repetition, consider Deuteronomy 30:2. You readily see *"thou mayest"* four times in this verse. Usually it is in a sermon that you hear this done for emphasis sake.

But, it is supposed, by this author, that the crowning example of repetition which is also time consuming and taxing on one's patience is found in Numbers chapter 7. In this long chapter of 89 verses, with the exception of the different tribes named, and their different leaders, for six whole verses, the same ingredients for an offering are given over, and over again. Just so the reader will appreciate it, one example, verses 12-17 will be cited here.

> *12 And he that offered his offering the first day was Nahshon the son of Amminadab, of the tribe of Judah: 13 And his offering was one silver charger, the weight thereof was an hundred and thirty shekels, one silver bowl of seventy shekels, after the shekel of the sanctuary; both of them were full of fine flour mingled with oil for a meat offering: 14 One spoon of ten shekels of gold, full of incense: 15 One young bullock, one ram, one lamb of the first year, for a burnt offering: 16 One kid of the goats for a sin offering: 17 And for a sacrifice of peace offerings, two oxen, five rams, five he goats, five lambs of the first year: this was the offering of Nahshon the son of Amminadab.*

Now, imagine reading that to the tune of 12 times, one time for each of the 12 tribes of Israel. Then, a recap, if you did not catch it the first time through, is given tabulating for each item times 12 for your understanding. But this is in addition to the instructions given in the opening verses of this chapter. Again, this is the way that the Biblical writers wrote in the Hebrew tongue, repetition for emphasis, understanding, exactness and accuracy, and faithfulness.

Everyone knows, that is if they have read anything in the Bible, almost anywhere therein are given names that are foreign to westerners to try and pronounce. How exhausting to read nearly the first nine chapters of First Chronicles with little other words it seems than names, page after page, after page. Lol. One is tempted to ask a few questions: "Why are these names given? Why are there so many names given?

Why could they not have shortened the names or something, and made them easier to pronounce?" Exactly, right? But what if the reasons are given in the text? Would that help you to see why these names are so important in the eastern culture? We read in 1 Chronicles 9:1,

> So all Israel were reckoned by genealogies;

There you have it. God used the chronicler to count Israel by tracing their genealogies, the family tree so to speak.

Further, the real Messiah, the Lord Jesus Christ's lineage can be traced back to Adam (Matt. 1:1-17; Lk. 3:23-38.) That my friend, shows even the worst critic who the true Messiah of Israel really is. How exciting! Do you see the continuity and the consistency of Holy Scripture? Ah, look again kind friend, till you see Him.

Proverbial Expressions

Now, there are oh so very many phrases used today which come right from off the pages of Holy Writ. The following are but a few of what we call 'Proverbial Phrases,' common among English speaking people.

> Gen. 3:19, *"In the sweat of thy face."* Not the sweat of your brow.
>
> Gen. 4:9, *"Am I my brother's keeper."*
>
> Gen. 30:27, *"I have learned by experience."*
>
> Gen. 31:37, *"Stuff,"* NOT the NIV's "goods." People ask, "Where's my stuff?"
>
> Ex. 2:13, *"Fellow"* for the yankees, but for southerners it's "feller" Isa 14:8.
>
> Ex. 23:13, *"Neither let it be heard out of thy mouth."*
>
> Num. 9:20, *"And so it was."*
>
> Num. 10:14, *"In the first place."*

Num. 13:18, *"What it is."*

Num. 22:31, *"And fell flat on his face."*
Deut. 2:14, *"Wasted."*

Deut. 24:8, *"By the way."*

Jos. 9:14, *"Victuals."*

Jos. 7:19, *"Tell me now, what thou hast done?"*

Jud. 12:3, *"I put my life in my hands."*

Jud. 15:8, *"He smote them hip and thigh."*

1 Sam. 20:1, *"What have I done?"*

Sam. 13:14, *"A man after his own heart."*

2 Sam. 1:19, *"How are the mighty fallen!"*

Sam. 12:7, *"Thou art the man."* 'You're the man.'

1 Kings 19:12, *"A still small voice."*

2 Kings 20:1, *"Sick unto death."*

2 Chron. 30:18, *"The good LORD pardon every one."*

2 Chron. 36:3, *"Put him down."* Not as the NIV has, *"dethrone him."* It means, you put him in his place.

Neh. 13:11, *"Set them in their place."* NOT NIV's "station in their post

Job 10:21, *"The shadow of death."*

Job 19:20, *"The skin of my teeth."* We mean, I barely escaped.

Ps. 90:9, *"A tale that is told."*

Ps. 90:10, *"Threescore years and ten."*

Ps. 107:27, *"At their wit's end."*

Prov. 4:25, *"Right on,"* NOT NIV's "fix your gaze."

Prov. 13:15, *"The way of the transgressor is hard."*

Prov. 27:1, *"Boast not thyself of to morrow."*

Eccl. 1:9, *"There is no new thing under the sun."*

Eccl. 3:20, *"All go unto one place."*

Isa. 6:5, *"Woe is me!"*

Isa. 22:13, *"Let us eat and drink; for to morrow we shall die."*

Isa. 40:15, *"As a drop of a bucket."*

Isa.53:7, *"As a lamb to the slaughter."*

Isa. 65:5, *"Holier than thou."* NOT NIV's "I am too sacred for you."

Jer. 2:21, *"Degenerate."*

Jer. 6:30, *"Reprobate."*

Micah 7:3, *"Wrap it up."*

Matt. 5:13, *"The salt of the earth."*

Matt. 23:24, *"Strain at a gnat."*

Lk. 12:1, *"In the mean time."*

Jn. 19:30, *"Gave up the ghost."*

Acts 4:19, *"Right in the sight of God."*

Acts 9:27, *"In the name of Jesus."*

Acts 10:6, *"What thou oughtest to do."*

Acts 27:34, *"This is for your health."*

Rom. 6:23, *"The wages of sin."*

Rom. 13:1, *"The powers that be."*

Rom. 13:8, *"Owe no man anything."*

2 Cor. 12:7, *"A thorn in the flesh."*

1 Thess. 1:3, *"Labour of love."*

1 Tim. 6:10, *"The root of all evil."*

It has been suggested that there are over 250 familiar phrases in the Bible. We speak like we read a King James Bible, not a New International Version (NIV), or any other modern version.

Hebraisms In The Old Testament Text

A man by the name of William Rosenau, wrote a book called, *HEBRAISMS IN THE AUTHORIZED VERSION OF THE BIBLE* which will be referenced somewhat in this section dealing with expressions used in the Bible. In the section dealing with so called Archaisms, there he gives the reader several words.

In Gen. 1:30, we read of "meat" instead of "food." Through the Bible we see words that we seldom use or hear used, such as: "shall" for "will," and "which" for "whom," "I pray thee" instead of "please." As in Gen. 24:12 we read, *"Send me good speed"* instead of "let me be met with success." The word "shew" is used instead of "tell" in many places throughout both testaments.

Now, there are places in the Bible where there are expressions, whether familiar or not, that may or may not be easy to understand. To be sure, the more we read the Bible the better they will be understood. However, they will be noted, at least some of them anyway, nonetheless. One is found in Numbers 33:55, speaking of Israel's enemies if not destroyed they will be

> *"Pricks in your eyes and thorns in your sides."*

What exactly does this mean? Well, this expression has a couple more just like it. For example, in Judges 2:3 we read,

> *Wherefore I also said, I will not drive them out from before you; but they shall be as thorns in your sides, and their gods shall be a snare unto you.*

Again, in 2 Corinthians 12:7 Paul said that,

> *there was given to me a thorn in the flesh, the messenger of Satan to buffet me, lest I should be exalted above measure.*

Honestly, it is much like the modern expression, "a pain in my neck." In Paul's case however, it was the *"messenger of Satan"* who was the *"thorn in the flesh."* But, as said above, the pricks, thorns, and snares were Israel's enemies and their gods which would get the upper hand and then God would have to judge them with the other nations. The enemies of Israel would use and abuse them and God would allow it because they should have driven these nations out of Canaan as they were told by God to do.

In Deuteronomy 32:10 another proverbial expression is used, *"The apple of his eye."* God keeps Israel as the apple of His eye is the meaning of the text. David says to God in Psalms 17:8,

> *"Keep me as the apple of the eye, hide me under the shadow of thy wings."*

There remains a couple more references that should be given before giving the meaning of this phrase. In Proverbs 7:2, we read,

> *Keep my commandments, and live; and my law as the apple of thine eye.*

In Lamentations 2:18 says,

> *Their heart cried unto the Lord, O wall of the daughter of Zion, let tears run down like a river day and night: give thyself no rest; let not the apple of thine eye cease.*

The expression is much like what Ezekiel's wife meant to him, *"The desire of thine eyes"* (Eze. 24:16). It is to be understood He kept him as his own eyes. What watchful care God has for His own people.

In 2 Kings 9:30, an unfamiliar phrase, to us anyhow, is used: *"And tired her head."* This expression simply means Jezebel adorned her head or hair, after putting on her make-up as women still do today. Some things never change, do they ladies? Really, the context would tell you what she was doing even though you may not be able to explain this phrase.

When a man named Jehu had come through the city of Jezreel, Jezebel quickly fixed herself up and looked out the window, not knowing of course he would call for her death and run over her himself which fulfilled a prophecy given years earlier by Elijah, the prophet of God. (See 2 Kings 9:10). No further comment is needed, the reader is encouraged to read the whole account given in 2 Kings chapter 9.

English Archaisms

Rosenau now moves to showing his readers the difference between Hebraisms and alleged English archaisms. In Genesis 25:8 is an English archaism, *"Gave up the ghost," and he died.*

There are many examples of alleged English archaisms which in their context the Scriptures yield the meaning with just a little study.

I John 1:1, *"That Which"* for "he whom or what was." Genesis 13:8, *"We be brethren,"* for "we are brethren."

Genesis 24:12, *"Send me good speed,"* for "let me be met with success."

Exodus 22:2, *"If a thief be found breaking up,"* for "breaking in."

Leviticus 2:4, *"An oblation of a meat offering,"* for "offering a meal offering."

Leviticus 8:7, *"Curious,"* for "skillfully wrought or worked."

Joshua 7:13, *"Against to-morrow"* for "tomorrow."

1 Samuel 19:4, *"Theeward"* for "thee, and you."

2 Kings 15:5, *"Several house"* for "quarantine."

1 Chronicles 16:6, *"Flesh"* for "meat."

2 Chronicles 28:25, *"Every several city"* for "every single city."

Esther 3:6, *"He thought scorn"* for "he was very angry."

Job 19:19, *"Inward friends"* for "confidential friends."

Psalms 18:18, *"Prevented me"* for "confronted me."

Isaiah 1:13, *"Cannot away with"* for "cannot bear."

Hosea 5:2, *"Are profound to make slaughter"* for "to have gone deep."

1 Corinthians 13:4, *(Charity) "vaunteth not itself"* for "does not boast."

The term "charity" will be dealt with in the next section of this book.

David Norton, in his book, *A Textual History of the King James Bible*, wrote on page 140,

> "The tendency of these guidelines is towards the preservation of archaisms that might otherwise be modernised. Archaisms were retained on purpose by the King James translators. Which should tell us that the King James Bible was 'archaic' when it was published in 1611."

Now, there's a thought to ponder dear reader, that the KJB was archaic before it was published, therefore, it was intentional by the translators themselves. What a great literary device to employ, archaism. Recall, *To Whom the Bell Tolls*, by Earnest Hemingway? The book is literally full of archaisms, and yet, it was nominated for a Pulitzer Prize. Also, we've all heard it said, "To thine own self be true," from Hamlet, by William Shakespeare. Figures of speech, many of them are archaic, yet still in use today. There are more words we think are archaic but used in England to this day. These will be dealt with in the last section of this book as well.

Now there remains one other matter to be briefly mentioned under archaic words, and that is the term, obsolete. Some words in our English Bible are not archaic, they're obsolete words. Vance, in his book, *Archaic Words and the Authorized Version*, on page 465, lists 20 of these words to give some idea of obsolete verb inflections. These will be given in our last section in Biblical English.

The fact of the matter is that all versions somewhere or another have archaic words, such as behold, maiden, unto, and warpt or comely to list only a few. One thing to be noted about being a KJB believer; it is highly important to be honest with our Bible and have honour and integrity at the same time.

One final example of an archaic word in the KJB. In Esther 7:4, "countervail" meaning to balance an action or to act against with equal force or simply to compensate.

Germanisms in the Text

There are not only Hebraisms, and alleged archaisms, but there are also what may be called Germanisms in the KJB. What is that you ask? An expression such as *"good courage"* in Deuteronomy 31:6, which is to say be strong, or be courageous. In Joshua 1:8 we read of *"good success."*

Since Martin Luther's German Bible is in the line of the KJB, we should not be surprised to see many Germanisms in our English Bible.

Let's consider a few more examples, shall we? In 1 Cor. 9:22 we read, *"To the weak became I,"* or in 2 Cor. 7:13, we see, *"exceedingly the more joyed we...."* In Psalms 46:2 we read, *"Therefore will not we fear,"* and in Ps. 56:10 we notice yet another Germanism, *"In God will I praise his word: in the LORD will I praise his word"* for I will praise.

In Acts 16:25 we see again the German influence for we read, *"Then departed Barnabas to Tarsus, for to seek Saul"* meaning that Barnabas went to Tarsus to find Saul.

Finally, in Acts 13:18, 44,

And about the time of forty years suffered he their manners in the wilderness...And the next sabbath day came almost the whole city together to hear the word of God.

God tolerated Israel's actions in the wilderness for forty years. None of these passages pose any difficulty to our understanding, it's just that the wording is arranged differently. There are of course many more examples of German influence in our beloved KJB, but it is hoped that these few passages will give you, the reader, some idea of their existence to better understand Holy Scripture.

Hebraisms In The New Testament Text

In Galatians 1:5, *"For ever and ever"* is another Hebraism influencing in the New Testament, and simply means "forever, and always". In Romans 7:3, *"(if) she be married to another man"* is to be understood as "if she is married to another man." Your mind will automatically make that adjustment just by reading the passage. By Hebraisms is meant the influence that the Hebrew language has over and is carried over into the English Bible (KJB). Consider, 2 Kings 2:3, *"Take away thy master from thy head"* means to "take your master (here it is Elijah) away from you."

Genesis 1:20, *"In the open firmament of*

heaven" means, "heavens, outer space, or the sphere of the stars." "The firmament...It is what strengthens or holds up and holds back the stars" (Vance, Laurence M., *Archaic Words and the Authorized Version*, Vance Publications, 1999, p. 139.) On the face of the expanse of heaven is a good way of understanding the text.

Genesis 21:12, *"In Isaac shall thy seed be called"* for "preserved, kept."

Joshua 6:26,

> He shall lay the foundation thereof in his firstborn, and in his youngest son shall he set up the gates of it.

This is understood to mean, laying the foundation of it shall cost him his firstborn, and the setting up of the gates shall cost him his youngest son.

Joshua 23:1, *"Well stricken in age"* means, "advanced in age, very old."

In Job 41:34, *"Children of pride"* or, "proud children."

Psalms 4:5, *"Sacrifices of righteousness"* or, "right sacrifices."

Psalms 60:3, *"Wine of astonishment"* is "staggering wine."

Conjunctions in the Text

One feature of the KJB which is literally all

over the place, it is annoying to some, redundant to others, and absolutely unacceptable for beginning sentences in English, is the oft repeated word "and."

Let's have two examples to suffice for the extensive use of "and" which literally comes from the Biblical languages in both Testaments. In The First Book Of Moses, called Genesis, will be our first example. Consider the word "And" in chapter one where all of the sentences except verses 1, and 27 out of 31 verses begin with "And."

Before citing a New Testament reference, if that seems odd, then read Leviticus 1:1, where a book opens with "And."

> AND the LORD called unto Moses, and spake unto him out of the tabernacle of the congregation, saying," (emphasis mine.)

The third Book of the KJB in the Old Testament begins with this conjunction *"And."* Why? It's to be connected with Exodus 40:34-38, which see.

The Gospel According to St. Matthew will be our second example of using this conjunction throughout and is a Hebraism which has influenced our KJB. Matthew 24:1,

> AND Jesus went out, and departed from the temple: and his disciples came to him for to shew him the buildings of the temple.

So, again, another chapter begins with the

word *"and,"* and is seen throughout this chapter in 16 verses. Furthermore, most of the other verses begin with connecting words such as, "For," "Then," "When," "So," and so on. This is mentioned so the reader of the KJB will not think that they are mistakes simply because we in the United States are told not to follow this example.

Reader, the word, "and" is used in at least two more ways in a KJB. Note, that in Gen. 2:3 and many more like it this conjunction can give repetition to expand and explain the meaning of a word. Consider, "created AND made" where "created" is defined as meaning "made." Finally, ponder Titus 2:13 where "and" is used to denote the Deity of Christ by the use of a figure of speech for emphasis called a hendiady: one through two. We have, *"the great God AND our Saviour Jesus Christ."* They are one and the same Person.

One particularly unique passage, to this another fellow Bible reader is Isaiah 40:27. For here we read,

> *Why sayest thou, O Jacob, and speakest,*
> *O Israel, My way is hid from the LORD,*
> *and my judgment is passed over from my*
> *God?*

So, did you catch what is going on in this passage? Read it again won't you, and see if you can identify this Hebraism? Maybe you can try and understand it by considering the word "Yea" after "Jacob" and before "speakest." In other words, Jacob and Israel are one and the same, and not different persons.

By the context of this verse your mind will make the necessary connection. Why sayest thou, O Jacob, yea, speakest, O Israel. Isn't God's word simply amazing and amazingly simple? That is, if we will spend time in it, it will amaze us as to what it says, and explain itself to us.

Another such example is also found in Isaiah, this time in 23:7. It reads,

> *Is this your joyous city, whose antiquity is of ancient days? her own feet shall carry her afar off to sojourn.*

"Antiquity is of ancient days." Seems harmless enough, right? It's like saying that your glory days are all in the past. Well, sort of like that, but not really. It is saying that your origin is ancient, from of old. This is reminiscent to this Bible believer of Micah 5:2, which is a prophecy of our Lord. It reads,

> *But thou, Beth-lehem Ephratah, though thou be little among the thousands of Judah, yet out of thee shall he come forth unto me that is to be ruler in Israel; whose goings forth have been from of old, from everlasting.*

Christ Jesus is from of old, yea from everlasting to everlasting. He is God after all, see Romans 9:5.

Parallelisms

Another literary device which should lend aid to answer the question, "What Can't I Understand My King James Bible?" is called Parallelism. Now according to Bishop Lowth, there are four different types of parallelisms, though today it's known as, Rhythm Of Thought In Succeeding Lines.

Synonymous Parallelism

The first type is Synonymous (repeating) Parallelism, where the second line repeats the thought of the first line but in a slightly different way. Consider, Psalms 8:4, which says,

"What is man, that thou art mindful of him?
and the son of man, that thou visitest him?"

See here, that the second line though somewhat repeating the thought of the first line, is different.

Can you dear reader, see the difference? God has shown that He is in fact mindful of man by visiting him. The shock to the Psalmist is the same in both questions that God would take note of puny man. "Man" in the first question is the same as "the son of man" in the second question, but it's different, isn't it? Mankind in general is the thought here before it plays out in either Adam or David. Adam could be the man mentioned in line one and David on the second line. Of God being "mindful" of man to visiting him is quite remarkable to say the least. God has visited man in creation, as well as redemption.

Note, this is also speaking of the God-Man, Christ Jesus. When you turn to Hebrews 2:6,

> *But one in a certain place testified, saying, What is man, that thou art mindful of him? or the son of man, that thou visitest him?*

You can see that the writer applies Psalm 8:4 to Jesus Christ. It's as though that man and the son of man meet together in Him.

The next passage to peruse is Psalm 19:7, where we read,

> *The law of the LORD is perfect, converting the soul: the testimony of the LORD is sure, making wise the simple.*

By now you know where this is going right? Both the "law" and "the testimony" are one and the same, its two ways of saying the same thing. It's a restatement but in a little different way. Both words, "law" and "testimony" are synonyms for the Scripture itself. "The law" is said to be "perfect", while the LORD'S "testimony" "is sure." "The law" converts while "the testimony" makes "wise." "The law" and "the testimony" are both *"of the LORD."*

These are synonymous with one another, yet different, and both the statements parallel one another in the same passage. Each describes what God's word is and pronounces what it effectively accomplishes. The same is true of Ps. 19:8; one writer says that both of these synonyms "statutes" and "commandment" looks upon God's word as orders, charges, and precepts. The word of God is seen as divine orders, they are "right" and "pure," they "rejoice the heart," they are "enlightening the eyes." Reader, see if you can look at the next verse and see them in light of the above thoughts. Remember, the second line repeats the first line, but in a different way.

In Psalms 51:7 we see that the principal words in the second line are synonyms of the corresponding words of the first line.

> *Purge me with hyssop, and I shall be clean: wash me, and I shall be whiter than snow.*

Or consider Isaiah 15:1, where we see it again,

> *The burden of Moab. Because in the night Ar of Moab is laid waste, and brought to silence; because in the night Kir of Moab is laid waste, and brought to silence;....*

The second line is repeated in a slightly variant form. The Isaiah passage is more of a reiteration honestly.

Synthetic Parallelism

The next example Bishop Lowth lists is called Synthetic (developing) Parallelism. This type of parallelism is where the second line builds up the thought of the first line. It is giving added thought on the same note. It differs from synonymous because it builds up the thought of the first line rather than repeating it differently.

An example would be Psalms 42:1:

As the hart panteth after the water brooks,
so panteth my soul after thee, O God.

This is a Simile (a figure of speech involving the comparison of one thing with another thing of a different kind, it's used to make a description more emphatic or vivid; as brave as a lion.), from nature.

In the psalmist's estimation, he is facing a severe divine drought. You know it's a simile because it uses "As" and "so." *"As the hart panteth" "so panteth my soul"* (emphasis mine.) The "hart" is panting after water, and the psalmist *"panteth after thee, O God."* The psalmist panting after God is built off of the example of the "hart" panting for water. As one pants so does the other pant. As an animal thirsts for water, the psalmist longs after, thirsts for God. He says that in the next verse, *"My soul thirsteth for God, for the living God: when shall I come and appear before God?"* We should all feel the same way friend.

Antithetic Parallelism

The third example listed is called, Antithetic (contrasting) Parallelism, where the second line gives the direct opposite of the first line. This should prove very interesting for it is seen in many Scriptures. Let's consider two such examples from the Bible. In

Proverbs 13:1 it says, *"A wise son heareth his father's instruction: but a scorner heareth not rebuke."* This verse is where the second line is introduced by a "but" as here or with a than. "But," in the KJB almost always introduces a contrast. The opposition is seen between a son who is wise because he hears and heeds his father's instruction, whereas one who is a scorner does not hear or heed when he is being rebuked. Do you see the opposites in this verse?

Look at Proverbs 15:17, which says,

Better is a dinner of herbs where love is,
than a stalled ox and hatred therewith.

The dinner in an atmosphere of love is better than having an ox raised in a stall for steaks where there is hatred. Better is a dish of herbs, than the best of beef served with hatred. The ox raised in a stall is fed with the best feed, and its meat is tender and delicious. Herbs are not vegetables as some versions would have you to believe.

Herbs are distinguished from vegetables because, like spices, they are used in small amounts to provide mostly flavor to food. However, herbs are plants used as food, they refer to a leafy part of a plant whether fresh or dried. Examples of herbs are: Basil, green onions, thyme, parsley, shrubs such as rosemary. Some plants are both herbs and spices, like dill weed or dill seed called coriander leaves and seeds. The coriander leaves were used as a salad, the fresh leaves are known as cilantro. The anise was used to flavor breads and cakes and aided in digestion. Bay leaves also alter the taste of stews and soups. Well, so much for a lesson in herbs used for food and as spices.

What came to mind with herbs and thinking of spices is a New Testament passage, Matthew 23:23. This is where the Lord is rebuking the scribes and Pharisees giving out *"Woes"* as He denounces them as *"hypocrites"* because as He says in verse 1, *"...for they say, and do not."*

So in verse 23, Jesus says to them and His audience,

> *Woe unto you, scribes and Pharisees, hypocrites! For ye pay tithe of mint and anise and cummin, and have omitted the weightier matters of the law, judgment, mercy, and faith: these ought ye to have done, and not to leave the other undone.*

Clearly, the tithe here is garden vegetables, commanded in Leviticus 27:30-32, of which was brought to the storehouse at Jerusalem once every three years according to: Deut. 14:28; 26:12; Malachi 3:10; Nehemiah 10:38. The point in bringing this up, is, of course, because the mint is like our mint, the anise is a dill-spice, and the cummin is an herb. (See Isaiah 28:25). Ah, interesting, their tithe was to be eaten, see Matt. 23:18-19. Enough said.

In Psalms 37:16 it states,

> *"A little that a righteous man hath is better than the riches of many wicked."*

The final example that will be cited at this time will be Proverbs 12:15,

> The way of a fool is right in his own eyes:
> but he that hearkeneth unto counsel is
> wise."

Stair-Like Parallelism

There are variations of the above types of parallelisms, but one is common enough to be called a fourth kind, which is Stair-like Parallelism. Stair-like parallelism is sometimes called chain-like parallelism in which a word or thought in one line is taken up or is expanded in the following lines so that it proceeds to a climax.

Let's look at some examples from Scripture. In Exodus 15:16, we read,

> Fear and dread shall fall upon them; by
> the greatness of thine arm they shall be as
> still as a stone; till thy people pass over, O
> LORD, till the people pass over, which
> thou hast purchased.

You can see that this verse follows a train of thought to its natural conclusion, right? First, notice that verses 16-17 is an expression of confidence in the promises of God which was made to Abraham some 700 years earlier according to Genesis 12:15-17 one writer reminds us. This is also a reference to Joshua 4:23 when Israel passed over the river Jordan.

Really, what you're dealing with here in this passage is the fear and dread of Israel on the

Canaanites because of their God, specifically the miracle that took place at the Red Sea.

Another example of this type of parallelism is found in passages such as Psalm 24:8, where again, a chain of events is leading up to a final conclusion.

> Who is this King of glory? The LORD strong and mighty, the LORD mighty in battle.

Or consider, Psalm 3:1-2, which states,

> LORD, how are they increased that trouble me! Many are they that rise up against me. Many there be which say of my soul, There is no help for him in God. Selah.

Unfamiliar Phrases/Clauses in the Text

Admittedly, there are at times unfamiliar phrases and or clauses, and that shall now occupy our attention in the quest to understand more of the English KJB. Consider 1 Corinthians 6:9, which says, *"Abusers of themselves with mankind."* It means to lie with, or to cohabit with, a male, literally, it's a reference to homosexuality. There are words that should be associated together along with this verse, such as "effeminate," "fornication," and "sodomy."

Then there is the phrase, *"superfluity of naughtiness"* in James 1:21, which really is an overflowing of evil or wickedness. The whole verse reads,

Wherefore lay apart all filthiness and superfluity of naughtiness, and receive with meekness the engrafted word, which is able to save your souls.

From 2 Corinthians 7:1 we can see the meaning of the phrase under consideration:

Having therefore these promises, dearly beloved, let us cleanse ourselves from all filthiness of the flesh and spirit, perfecting holiness in the fear of God.

Usually the word "superfluity" is translated as "abundance," but sometimes it is other words close in meaning, such as "shall exceed" (Matthew 5:20), "that remained" (Mtt. 14:20), "remained over and above" (John 6:13.), while "naughtiness" is "evil" (Mtt. 6:34), "malice" (1 Cor. 5:8), "wickedness" (Acts 8:22), and "maliciousness" (Romans 1:29). Again, if the reader can get into the habit of looking at the first appearance of a word and follow it through the Scriptures, the context will always yield the meaning of whatever you're searching out.

What about the phrase in this passage, Numbers 23:10?

Who can count the dust of Jacob, and the number of the fourth part of Israel? Let me die the death of the righteous, and let my last end be like his!

My, this is not so bad, to be sentenced to death; to deserve the death sentence. You see, Balaam wanted to die like a righteous man, but when you live a selfish life as he did, it probably will not happen. It did not, for we see from Numbers 31:8 that he died *"with a sword."* Though some righteous people die in this way, Balaam was not righteous by a long shot. At least not according to New Testament sources such as 2 Peter 2:15; Jude 11 which states this,

> *"and ran greedily after the error of Balaam for reward,"*

Revelation 2:14 says,

> *...the doctrine of Balaam, who taught Balac to cast a stumblingblock before the children of Israel, to eat things sacrificed unto idols, and to commit fornication.*

Balaam was not a righteous man, rather, he *"loved the wages of unrighteousness."* That is certainly not a description of a righteous man.

The following will be a short list and explanation of seemingly unfamiliar Biblical Expressions.

In the following references in the Bible: (Numbers 35:12; Deuteronomy 19:6, 12; Joshua 20:3, 5, 9), we have the expression *"of avenger of blood"*), while in Numbers 35:19, 21, 24-25, 27; 2 Samuel 14:11 we read the interchangeable term *"the revenger of blood."*

We understand that today these terms are different. It is the avenger who gets his revenge on his enemy. So, it is for this reason these two phrases have been chosen to be included in this second section of Biblical Expressions. Again, the context gives the clues necessary to know the meaning, but in case someone has not picked-up on it, it is given here.

The teaching from the Holy Scriptures is that if someone accidently murders another person with no premeditation in his heart or if it was in self-defense, the guilty individual may flee to one of the six cities of refuge and be safe. He was required to remain in that city until the death of the High Priest. But if he did not take heed to this requirement, the *"avenger of blood"* who is the next of kin to the victim would become *"the revenger of blood"* and kill him. No doubt the victim's family member would find out who the killer was and in what city of refuge he was residing and waited for a chance to even the score to "avenge" the death of his loved one.

> And the angel of the LORD found her" (Hagar) "by a fountain of water in the wilderness, by the fountain in the way to Shur (Genesis 16:7).

Vance tell us that this phrase *"the angel of the LORD"* is found 59 times in 58 verses throughout 11 Old Testament books and 3 New Testament books. But what does it mean?

In Genesis 16 it is abundantly clear that this particular angel is the Lord Jesus Christ, a Pre-incarnate appearance, that is, in the flesh long before His birth which is recorded in the New Testament.

We know that this is the Lord because the following verses spell it out for the reader. In verses 9-10 we read,

> And the angel of the LORD said unto her, Return to thy mistress, and submit thyself under her" (Sarai) "hands. And the angel of the LORD said unto her, I will multiply thy seed exceedingly, that it shall not be numbered for multitude.

This tells us that this angel is the Lord because he says, "I will multiply thy seed." In verse 11 this angel says something that only God can do, "multiply thy seed." Further, this angel predicts the child's future when He says in verse 12,

> And he will be a wild man; his hand will be against every man, and every man's hand against him; and he shall dwell in the presence of all his brethren.

Then Hagar says something that identifies this Angel in verse 13,

> "And she called the name of the LORD that spake unto her, Thou God seest me: for she said, Have I also here looked after him that seeth me?"

This phrase always implies Deity in angelic form, but what about the case of Judges 13:16? The verse reads,

> And the angel of the LORD said unto Manoah, Though thou detain me, I will not eat of thy bread: and if thou wilt offer a burnt offering, thou must offer it unto the

*LORD. For Manoah knew not that he was
an angel of the LORD.*

There is good indication in how this angel
makes his exit from earth and that He is, in point of
fact, Deity.

Consider, verses 18-19,

*And the angel of the LORD said unto him,
Why askest thou thus after my name,
seeing it is secret? So Manoah took a did
with a meat offering, and offered it upon a
rock unto the LORD: and the angel did
wondrously; and Manoah and his wife
looked on.*

This Angel is referred to as *"the angel of his
presence"* in Isaiah 63:9 because that text goes on to
say about Him, that He would

*"save them: in his love and in his pity he
redeemed them; and he bare them, and
carried them all the days of old."*

Clearly, this is a reference to Deity, and is here
identified as God Himself.

Also, it needs to be added, that there are times
that a capital letter is used, as in Exodus 23:20,

*Behold, I send an Angel before thee"
(Israel) "to keep thee in the way, and to
bring thee into the place which I have
prepared.*

Now, this is Deity because according to the
next few verses God Himself declares it. God says of
Him that He can pardon transgressions, and only God

can do this says, Luke 5:21,

> And the scribes and the Pharisees began to reason, saying, Who is this which speaketh blasphemies? Who can forgive sins, but God alone.

As stated above, this writer believes this Angel to be the Lord Jesus Christ, a pre-incarnate appearance in human form before His virgin birth recorded in the New Testament. The reason for this conclusion on the author's part is due to several factors. For one, since this Angel is an appearance of God Himself, the theologians call it a Theophany.

Next, when thinking about God the Father, it is not proper to think that He would take on a human form; He is God and Father. The way that He is described in Revelation 4:2-3 just would not lend support that He'd be this Angel of the LORD, He would be the LORD spoken of in the Bible.

> And immediately I was in the spirit; and, behold, a throne was set in heaven, and one sat on the throne. And he that sat was to look upon like a jasper and a sardine stone: and there was a rainbow round about the throne, in sight like unto an emerald.

Then too, it surely would not be God the Holy Ghost, as He is described in Scripture as "wind" (Ezekiel 37:6), and "breath" (Eze. 37:9), and "spirit" (Eze. 37:14). In Genesis 1:2, it reads in part, "...And the Spirit of God moved upon the face of the waters."

He is further referred to as *"the breath of the Almighty"* (Job 33:4), and again in Psalms 33:6 as *"the breath of his mouth."*

Therefore, this leaves God the Son, the Lord Jesus Christ as the only logical, Scriptural and theological Person as the Angel of the Lord. Consider, John 1:14, which says,

> And the Word was made flesh; and dwelt among us, (and we beheld his glory, the glory as of the only begotten of the Father,) full of grace and truth.

That is, Jesus became flesh. Therefore it is conceivable that since this was to be, He would be the probable One to make PRE-INCARNATE appearances in the Old Testament. All will agree that with all the O.T. prophecies of Him coming to dwell among us in the flesh, such as Isaiah 7:14, it is not inconceivable for Him to be the only One who could be the Angel of the Lord.

In Genesis 23:21 it is written that this Angel has God's *"name in him"* as Matthew 1:23 has it, *"they shall call his name Emmanuel, which being interpreted is, God with us."* Hopefully you get the point as to the identity of this Angel as the Lord Jesus Christ.

In 1 Timothy 6:20 we have yet another expression to consider. What does *"profane and vain babblings"* mean? The whole verse reads:

> O Timothy, keep that which is committed to

> *thy trust, avoiding profane and vain babblings, and oppositions of science falsely so called.*

This verse is close in meaning with 1 Timothy 1:6 which reads, *"From which some having swerved have turned aside unto vain jangling."* These passages are connected to such verses as 2 Tim. 2:16; Titus 1:10. While "vain" is understood as "empty," and "without meaning" and "babbling" means "noise" (Rev. 6:1), "jangling" on the other hand means "wrangling, and quarreling." From Titus 1:10 we see that it means "vain talkers." It is also "vain babblings." See, once and again dear reader the KJB defines itself. Praise the Lord!

In Numbers 5:12-13 we find another interesting phrase.

> *Speak unto the children of Israel, and say unto them, If any man's wife go aside, and commit a trespass against him, And a man lie with her carnally, and it be hid from the eyes of her husband, and be kept close, and she be defiled, and there be no witness against her, neither she be taken with the manner.*

So, here is the phrase, *"she be taken with the manner."* This is very unique to say the least. This, from the context, is dealing with the act of adultery, and she is not found out, no one saw her, and she does not become pregnant from this illegitimate act. Some say that this expression comes from a thief taken with stolen items found in his possession.

The end of verse 13 can be understood as she is taken with the very act itself or she was taken in the act and her husband became suspicious of her cheating, so he has a ritual performed to determine if she were guilty. In John 8:3 we read,

> *"And the scribes and Pharisees brought unto him a WOMAN TAKEN IN ADULTERY;"* (emphasis mine) *"and when they had set her in the midst."*

Let's consider another passage in Proverbs 30:20,

> *"Such is the way of an adulterous woman; she eateth, and wipeth her mouth, and saith, I have done no wickedness."*

In any case, it must also be remembered that she was taken with the manner or had to be subjected to this ceremony to determine her guilt.

What about the phrase *"the abomination of desolation"* found in Matthew 24:15? Well, if you look and read the Old Testament references, maybe it would yield light or perhaps not. But let's list them for studying purposes: Daniel 8:13; 9:27; 11:31; 12:11; Matthew 24:15. Then considering that it is also written, *"the abomination that maketh desolate."*

But real light is shed on this phrase when you read a cross reference in 2 Thessalonians 2:4,

> *"Who* ("the son of perdition" v.3) *opposeth and exalteth himself above all that is called God, or that is worshipped; so that he as God sitteth in the temple of God, shewing*

himself that he is God."

However, let it be understood that according to Daniel 9:27, the Antichrist causes the sacrifice to stop and sets up an image of himself or enters and defiles the temple of the Jews in the holy of holies and declares that he is God instead of Jehovah being God. This is an abomination; so, by doing this, he desecrates the rebuilt temple. In Jeremiah 16:18 it says *"detestable and abominable things,"* therefore, what is an abomination is detestable, something of disgust and is hated.

> *And thou shalt put in the breastplate of judgment the Urim and the Thummim; and they shall be upon Aaron's heart, when he goeth in before the LORD: and Aaron shall bear the judgment of the children of Israel upon his heart before the LORD continually.* (Exodus 28:30).

"Urim and the Thummim" are mentioned in Leviticus 8:8; Numbers 27:21; Deuteronomy 33:8; 1 Samuel 28:6; Ezra 2:63; Nehemiah 7:65, and may be connected with divination as the breastplate and "birth stones" were connected with Biblical Astrology. You see, to say, as some have, that these merely gave a "yes" or a "no" does not go along with Scripture. For in 1 Samuel 30:8 when God answered David, He did so with a sentence.

> *And David enquired at the LORD, saying, Shall I pursue after this troop? Shall I overtake them? And he answered him,*

*Pursue: for thou shalt surely overtake
them, and without fail recover all.*
(emphasis mine).

Now, it is not to be assumed by the above explanations that you should use a modern translation instead of the King James Bible, as if to give the impression that they do not need to be explained. A FEW examples from the New International Version of the Bible, the New King James Version of the Bible, the New American Standard Version of the Bible, the Holman Christian Standard Bible (version of the Bible), and, finally, the Contemporary English Version of the Bible could be shown to have expressions that are peculiar.

How about considering the following carpenters terms: soffit, fascia, mullion, sash, sill, gable, and ridge? They certainly need an explanation to the average person who is unfamiliar with the world of carpentry. What does the reader make of the following lawyer terms? Would a law firm or law school allow and update words, just to prove why they should be relics of the past? Here are just a few examples of their terms: Answer, appearance, rest, stay temporary, moving party, movant, lockout, lien, pray, Habeas Corpus, nolle, pleadings, judicial proceeding, pro se, voir dire, nolo contendere, trial de novo, challenge, and order. Since they will not revise them, the public must either learn these terms or have them explained on a need to know basis.

Therefore, dear reader, please do not be alarmed

that our King James Bible has words that may need an explanation in order to better understand God's words. All professions have "tradesman terms" that need explanation to the beginner. Clues will be given in this book to further help the Bible reader to better understand the Holy Scriptures. Again, continuous reading of the Bible, the law of first mention of a word, following the use of the word through the text, or a good dictionary, such as *AMERICAN DICTIONARY OF THE ENGLISH LANGUAGE* by Noah Webster, 1828 will be a great source of information.

BIBLICAL ENGLISH

Biblical English

Biblical English, or the English language used in the King James Bible, is a providential language raised up as a special vehicle for the work of spreading the word of God among all nations, especially the English-speaking ones.

In The Epistle Dedicatory, we read in part,

> For when Your Highness had once out of deep judgment apprehended how convenient it was, that out of the Original Sacred Tongues, together with comparing of the labours, both in our own, and other foreign Languages, of many worthy men who went before us, there should be one more exact Translation of the holy Scriptures into the English Tongue;....

> The first and fourteenth, because they directly relate to the subject at hand, are here given in full.

> 1. The ordinary Bible read in the church, commonly called the Bishops' Bible, to be followed, and as little altered as the truth of the original will permit.

> 14. These translations to be used when they agree better with the next than the Bishops' Bible, viz. Tindalls', Matthews', Coverdale's, Whitchurch's, Geneva[4].

---

[4] Laurence Vance, King James: His Bible, and its Translators, p.84.

In other words, they had Tyndale's Bible (1525-1535), Matthew's Bible (1537), Coverdale's Bible (1532-1537), the Great Bible (printed by Whitchurch in 1549), the Geneva Bible (1560), and the Bishop's Bible (1568), which were to be used if they agree with the original Biblical Languages (Hebrew, Aramaic, and Greek). These six English Bibles helped produce the seventh and final English Bible, the King James. So, the Authorized Version meets the criteria of Psalm 12:6 that the Lord's words were *"purified seven time*[5]

Doctor A.T. Robertson in his monumental work, *A Grammar of the Greek New Testament: In Light Of Historical Research*, (Broadman Press, Nashville, 1934) p.92, writes,

> No one to-day speaks the English of the King James Version, or ever did for that matter, for, though like Shakespeare, it is the pure Anglo-Saxon, yet, unlike Shakespeare, it reproduces to a remarkable extent the spirit and language of the Bible. As Luther's German Bible largely made the German language, so the King James Version has greatly affected modern English (both vernacular and literary).

Later Robertson writes,

> The point is that the N.T. writers were open to Semitic influence.

---

[5] Vance, King James: His Bible, And Its Translators, Vance Publications, Pensacola, FL, 2006, p. 84.

Then the point made thus far is that the KJB is the seventh English Bible according to the rules given them and is the purified Bible. It then follows that when considering the third section or division of this book, Why Can't I Understand My King James Bible? That, says Robertson, "No one to-day...or ever did for that matter," speak like the KJB does.

This therefore means, dear reader, that the KJB was archaic even for its time. It was meant to be written this way from the very start of the translation project. The KJB has been open to and contains Semitic or Hebrew influences, and as such is different from any modern version. It therefore follows, my friends, that the KJB does not agree with the modern version philosophy, that it should be written in today's style of language.

This is, I submit to you the reader the word and words of God, the Holy Bible for us today. They did not write it to be in the language of their day. Rather, it is written in an endearing and enduring style to last forever. As they wrote and as given above,

> "...there should be one more exact Translation of the holy Scriptures into..."

Question: Does this mean that since the Revision Revised, until the present hour, that each additional version is silently saying, one more exact translation into English, and one more, and one more, and one more to the tune of over 200 English translations?

When will this version of the month satisfy every English reader? Surely, this craze of "I need another version to help me understand the Bible" has to stop at some point? Are we becoming so lazy and irreverent towards God's word that we will continue this dumbing down of the Holy Bible so that no one reads and studies the Scriptures for there will be no need?

The newest and up-to-date version will no longer need God, much less seek Him. But Genesis 40:8 records the words of Joseph saying, *"Do not interpretations belong to God?"* Granted that we need to be able to read the Bible, but anyone can get out of the KJB what they need to get out of it. Let's consider a passage to support this thought.

In Romans 16:25-26,

Now to him that is of power to stablish you according to my gospel, and the preaching of Jesus Christ, according to the revelation of the mystery, which was kept secret since the world began, But now is made manifest, and BY THE SCRIPTURES OF THE PROPHETS, according to the commandment of the everlasting God, MADE KNOWN TO ALL NATIONS FOR THE OBEDIENCE OF FAITH. (emphasis mine).

God makes His words known to all nations in order that they may be saved.

Consider John 20:30-31,

And many other signs truly did Jesus in

> the presence of his disciples, which are not written in this book; But these are written, that ye might believe that Jesus is the Christ, the Son of God; and that believing ye might have life through his name.

So, again, the Scriptures are given so that the lost can believe on Christ and be saved.

In *The King James Version Defended*, by distinguished scholar Dr. Edward Hills, (Christian Research Press, Des Moines, 1956) he writes on page 218 Fourth Edition 1984 and Reprint 1988,

> In the first place, the English of the King James Version is not the English of the early 17th century. To be exact, it is not a type of English that was ever spoken anywhere. It is biblical English, which was not used on ordinary occasions even by the translators who produced the King James Version.

Hills then quotes H. Wheeler Robinson and he adds that W. A. Irwin agrees with him, that,

> The King James Version,...owes its merit, not to the 17th-century English-which was very different-but to its faithful translation of the original. Its style is that of the Hebrew and of the New Testament Greek. Even in their use of thee and thou the translators were not following 17th-century English usage but biblical usage, for at the time these translators were doing their work these singular forms had already

been replaced by the plural you in polite conversation.

However, that one may see them here and there must be noted. On the next page Hills goes on to ask,

"What is the language of today?"

No one ever seems to define or qualify it. Besides, even the language of "today" will change from year to year. He adds,

"But in contrast, to these absurdities the language of the King James Version is enduring diction which will remain as long as the English language remains, in other words, throughout the foreseeable future."

Amen.

Hills then writes that those who promote modern-speech versions discourage memorizing of Scripture by promoting newer up-to-date translations. Compounded to that point, the speech of modern versions is unhistorical and irreverent. Still yet,

"the Bible is not a modern, human book," rather, "an ancient, divine Book."

He then opines:

...modern-speech Bibles are unscholarly. The language of the Bible has always savored of the things of heaven rather than the things of earth.

Reader, there is great reason to go to great lengths to bring out Hills argument and thus this writer as well, and that is the subject matter of this section; Biblical English which is unlike any other language on earth. As such, it will read differently than what we are accustomed to reading whether yesterday, today, or tomorrow. If this is true, no wonder some may experience moderate difficulty in reading the King James Bible for the first time through. It is Biblical English or as some refer to it as "the Kings English."

With that said; we will now deal with Biblical English in an effort to try and see if the reader can be helped by this study. Wanting the language of the Bible, the language of devotion and worship, to read like current writings is a fairly new concept. The Bible is of supernatural origins. It should be set apart as sacred and divine so as to demand our utmost when reading it with waiting dependence upon God for light and understanding.

What is meant by Biblical English? Well the King James Bible of course is Biblical English, radically different from all modern speech Bibles. Pretty much anywhere you read in the Bible the reader will notice the way the English is written. We've never read anything quite like the Bible anywhere else on this planet. In fact, if you attend a church where another version is read besides the Authorized Version of 1611 remarks like, "That doesn't even sound like the Bible," will be heard in many cases.

This is because the English of the KJB is absolutely unmistakable. It has been ingrained, yea embedded, into our country, our churches, and our consciences for over four centuries. It is my desire in this section to deal with Biblical English, British Spelling, and Brings Understanding which we know that light is from the words of the Bible and language from words of the British people. What is important is reading, meditating, studying, and praying in order to understand the word(s) of God.

Consider some examples of Biblical English from the pages of the Holy Bible itself which brings about our understanding of it.

There seems to be at this point for the writer no better way to begin with than what is called, in Gail Riplinger's book, *The Language of the King James Bible*, on page 95, "Fronting." That means bringing the middle or the end of a sentence to the front for emphasis. Then she references my favorite verse to quote, Hebrews 1:1-2,

> *God, who at sundry times and divers manners spake in time past unto the fathers by the prophets, Hath in these last days spoken unto us by his Son, whom he hath appointed heir of all things, by whom also he made the worlds;....*

My, this is indeed a fun and meaningful passage to quote. In fact, it is jammed packed with tremendous theological truth. You see, God at different times in the past, in diverse manners or ways, spoke to the forefathers of Israel by His prophets directly by an audible voice, visions or dreams. He also spoke indirectly, by signs, wonders, and miracles, communicating His plans and His purpose to the fathers. But it was always the word(s) of God He made known.

Now God speaks in these last days by His Son who is the heir to all things spoken of in Scripture. Consider: Psalms 2:7-8; 22:22-31; Rom. 8:17-23; Rev. 2:25-27 for starters.

Another thought contained in the Hebrews reference is Acts 4:12, where we read,

> *Neither is there salvation in any other: for there is none other name under heaven given among men, whereby we must be save.*

See John 3:16; 1:12-13; Matt. 1:21. If you think that this is all that is in the above passage, then by all means, stop. But for those of you with enquiring minds, consider further the following passages: John 5:22; Matt. 28:18-20 and Acts 17:30-31. But don't stop yet until you spend some time searching Col. 1:16-29; Ps. 78:38-39 and Lk. 1:30-33, and the list goes on and on. You will have to research Gentile conversion since Calvary, all the way to the reigning *"with Christ a thousand years"* in Revelation 20:4-7. But dear reader, there is much more, so why stop now? Enough is enough lest both of us grow weary as Ecclesiastes 12:12 tells us. What a wonderful study.

Archaic Words Or Obsolete?

As mentioned earlier, obsolete words are not archaic words. Vance list words like: couldest, shouldest, lovedst, creepeth, believeth, to give a few obsolete words. Probably you the reader might be tempted to think that these words and others like them are archaic and hard to be understood. But you would be wrong with such thinking. They are obsolete verb inflections, that is, we no longer in the English language inflect words like these and others like them. We actually have few inflections in our language, though Greek and Latin are highly inflected. By inflected, what is meant exactly?

English verbs are inflected to see the tense such as past, present and future. Figuring out whether the voice is active, passive or middle, who does the action or is acted upon. Such as, John hit the ball. Well, obviously, the ball received the action, etc. The mood shows the manner in which an action is to be expressed, and there are few different kinds of moods. We'll forbear comments here on our many types of moods as humans which is not what is being dealt with here. There also needs to be discovered in a word what's called number, such as, first, second or third person. Finally, in inflected verbs there is what's called person, which is whether a verb is singular or plural. Look, all of those things are done by grammarians to show that the words previously mentioned and a few others had some special inflections or word spellings in both the 2nd and 3rd

person singular.

Now reader, when you come across words in your Bible with an -est or st suffix (on the end of verbs), it is the second person singular. That means it's the one spoken to. Also, when you come across a verb with an ending (suffix) as -eth or th (the one spoken about), it is the third person singular. Vance makes a great point everyone, since Hebrew and Greek inflect verbs and this still exists in English in the second and third person singular, why is that a problem when our KJB does the same thing? Friend, it's really not that hard. It's just a matter of getting used to reading words with these endings.

In Luke 15:29-32 we find the use of personal pronouns beginning with T which is a singular pronoun. They are: Thou, Thy, Thee, and Thine, used in the Prodigal Son parable:

> *And he answering said to his father, Lo, these many years do I serve thee, neither transgressed I at any time thy commandment: and yet thou never gavest me a kid, that I might make merry with my friends: But as soon as this thy son was come, which hath devoured thy living with harlots, thou hast killed for him the fatted calf. And he said unto him, Son, thou art ever with me, and all that I have is thine. (Emphasis mine)*

Dr. Phil Stringer, in his pamphlet, *Biblical English*, gives some Biblical English Terms on page 11. Thou and Ye designates the subject of the verb.

While Thee and You designate the object of a verb. All of the terms with a T (thou, thy, thee, thine) are all singular personal pronouns. The terms with a Y (ye, you, yours) are plural personal pronouns.

Finally, he gives the two terms Shall and Will. Shall refers to the first person with the future tense, and the word Will refers to the second or third person in the future. An example comes from Mrs. Riplinger, "I shall drown and no one will save me."

In Luke 1:31-35 there are a number of "shalls," twelve to be exact. Then in Numbers 16:5 we read of a few "wills."

> *And he spake unto Korah and unto all his company, saying, Even to morrow the LORD will shew who are his, and who is holy; and will cause him to come near unto him: even him whom he hath chosen will he cause to come near unto him. (Emphasis mine)*

Our English Bible is a legal document; it deals with testaments and covenants, therefore, it should be expected to have legal language inside of it. For instance, words like: thereof, whereof, thereby, therein, hereby, herein, whereby, wherein, and wherefore. These terms are not archaisms by any means; rather they are legal terms which are still in use today. See page 93 above for a reminder of legal terms that are still in use today which many of us have no idea what they mean without a dictionary.

The following idea came to me as I read on Dr.

James H. Sightler's website. Sightler was dealing with 'Why The English Of The King James Bible Is Better Than That Of All The Modern Versions." The modifications made by this author reflect what is necessary to write at this point and time, but let the reader decide for himself.

(www.sightlerpublications.com)

1. Precise Reverent Pronouns

2. Poetic Rhythm Patterns

3. Proper Reflected Pronunciations

Precise Reverent Pronouns

The pronouns used in the KJB are necessary for accurate and an authoritative translation. Someone has aptly said that even in Gresham Machen in his book on Greek grammar, *New Testament Greek For Beginners*, he recognized that the second person singular and plural forms need the Thou, Thee, Thine, Thy, and the Ye, and You, and Your(s). Many recognize that these pronouns show reverence as well as reference to Deity. Reader, just know as many writers have said, all the pronouns that begin with the letter T are singular, while the pronouns beginning with the letter Y are plural.

Poetic Rhythm Patterns

One needs only to consider John 3:16 to see that ONLY in the KJB is this universal verse rhythmic, thus making it easy for memorization.

For God/ so/ loved the world,/ that/ he gave/ his only/ begotten Son,/ that/ whosoever believeth/ in him/ should not perish,/ but have/ everlasting life. (Emphasis mine)

No other modern version reads like our beloved English Bible.

Consider, 1 Samuel 30:31,

And to them which were in Hebron, and to all the places where David himself and his men WERE WONT TO HAUNT. (Emphasis mine).

Again, see the poetical flow in this part of the verse is missed when you "update" the language. This is an archaic English word for used to or accustomed to and could remind us of where "wont" is used again in Acts 16:13, which reads,

And on the sabbath we went out of the city by a river side, where prayer was wont to be made; and we sat down, and spake unto the women which resorted thither.

Here, "wont" means usually, habitually, or customary.

Proper Reflected Pronunciations

We have previously mentioned inflected words when dealing with the difference between Obsolete and Archaic words but can easily fit here as well. Thus, by accurately translating these pronouns and using the suffixes listed above, the KJB is vastly superior to other modern versions hands down. The reader should never be made to feel that his or her Bible is somehow inferior to the others. So, here consider that Biblical English is still around, but only in the KJB.

Let's consider a very interesting passage which has a word that those who criticize it do not understand. May we be able to see this word, though we do not use it today in normal conversation unless we reference a verse using it. This word, two words actually, is "only begotten" which comes from one Greek word though it is a compound word. So, when modern versions say, "one and only," they are only translating half of the Greek word.

Let's consider this word, shall we? If a meaning is given in Scripture to these two words *"only begotten"* then ponder Genesis 49:3,

> *Reuben, thou art my firstborn, my might, and the beginning of my strength, the excellency of dignity, and the excellency of power.*

In several New Testament passages the Lord Jesus is called the "firstborn" such as in: Mt. 1:25; Lk. 2:7; Rom. 8:29; Col. 1:15, 18; Heb. 11:28; 12:23. *"Firstbegotten"* is in Hebrews 1:6; Rev. 1:5. *"Firstfruits"* is used of Christ too, in 1 Cor. 15:20, 23.

When you update any of these terms, you lose the Old Testament connections to Christ. The same thing applies to "only begotten." Consider the following: "begotten" in Heb. 1:5 (Christ), and Heb.11:17, "only begotten" (Isaac) from the O.T. book, Genesis 22 who was a type of Christ. The KJB is consistent in all these references so you will get the connection to Christ.

Now, it is this authors belief that Christ is the eternal Son of God, for a couple of reasons but for now, let's just say that He is called "Son" in the O.T. long before His birth to a virgin named Mary in the N.T. Called "virgin" because she was found with child of the Holy Ghost as Mat. 1:20 and Lk. 1:35 tells us. Of course, later, she and Joseph had children together says Mat. 13:55-56. Jesus did not become the Son of God when He was the firstborn Son to Mary as some teach today.

To begin with, there are a number of Greek-English lexicons which define the Greek word as translated in the KJB as *"only begotten."* It is not my purpose to go into lexicons and Greek and/or Hebrew words in this book. But a question that may surface is something like, "Where did the KJB translators get this word, only begotten?" In 1395 the Wycliffe Bible, the first so-called Bible to be written in English, has only begotten Son, "'oon bigetun sone."

Tyndale used it in 1525, so did Coverdale in 1535, The Great Bible (Cranmer) in 1540, The Bishops' Bible in 1568, The Geneva Bible in 1587, Douay-Rheims in 1610 has it, and the list goes on up to the ASV in 1901, then the NKJV of 1982 has it, and so does the NAB of 1995, and also the Knox Bible of 2012. The Catholic Douay Bible of 1950 has "only begotten" in it.

Then in 1970 and 1985, Catholic Bibles read, "His only Son" in John 3:16. Some versions of the Bible read "only unique Son" or "one and only Son." What's the problem the reader asks? One, as said above, is that the Doctrine of the Eternal Sonship of Christ is affected. But also, the truth that the Lord Jesus is NOT the ONLY SON of God.

In Job 1:6; 2:1 and 38:7 angels are called "sons of God." Not only that, but there are other references to children of God being sons of God in Jn. 1:12 and First John 5:1 which are believers as also "my sons and daughters," in 2 Cor. 6:18. So, what is the solution friend?

Did you know that in the Greek language there's a different word for unique and only begotten which has been around for say, 2,000 years? Therefore, as the Greek words are not the same, even so the two words unique and only begotten are not the same. My, isn't that something to know? But, the Greek word translated as only begotten has always meant just that.

Your KJB is Biblical English and is right. But, we must hasten to add, that the Lord Jesus Christ is the "only begotten" by being the only One directly begotten in the flesh by the Father. We, on the other hand, are adopted into His family when we believe the Gospel as outlined in 1 Corinthians 15:1-4.

In John 14:2, "IN my FATHER'S HOUSE ARE MANY MANSIONS: if it were not so, I would have told you. I go to prepare a place for you." (Emphasis mine)

In a computer conversation with Dr. Kirk DiVietro, "Mr. Computer," gave a passage of Scripture when he thinks of John. 14:2 from the O.T. Book of Daniel.

Daniel 4:30, which says,

The king spake, and said, Is not this great Babylon, that I have built for THE HOUSE OF THE KINGDOM by the might of my power, and for the honour of my majesty?

The thinking is "the house" matching "house" of Jn. 14:2. First you have the house of his kingdom that Babylon was built for, so Jesus says, "IN my Father's HOUSE," Heaven is God's house and in it *"are many mansions."*

The reading "mansion" goes back to other Bibles in English, to Tyndale. It even goes back over 1,000 years in old Latin, the vulgate, Raiment, and other ancient versions. What a tradition, a history that mansion enjoys! It did not originate with the KJB translators. There's a wild thought, the translators did not invent a word out of thin air, but used a word that's been around for many centuries.

This book is not about defining all the words of the KJB that you, the reader, feel needs to be addressed. Somewhere, at the end of this book will be a section listing places where you might go on the internet or purchase a book which will define the term in question. This book is a kind of 'how to' book to aid the reader in their quest to get more out of their Bible and to get into their Bible. Usually, a book that you purchase does not list the word that you need defined.

So, for the last two terms for this section, let's consider a word not used very much but which is worth mentioning. Can you pronounce this word? It is called, "concupiscence", and that definitely is not an everyday common word, is it? How is it used in the Bible?

Consider please, Romans 7:8, which says,

"But sin, taking occasion by the commandment, wrought in me all manner of concupiscence. For without the law sin was dead."

Wow, what a word! It is found in only two other places in our English Bible.

Let, me say this to you dear reader, that in this writer's library is a book simply called, *Single Syllable Words*, by Samuel C. Gipp, Ph.D. He has shown that there are 916 verses in our KJB where there were entire passages made up of only single syllable words. Gipp says that he went through the Bible some 10 times and marked them. Now, that is difficult to grasp for some, but wait, there's more. He wanted to know how other modern versions handled these verses. So he chose 7 modern versions, and guess what he found? Did they maintain those 916 single syllable verses as found in an archaic out-of-date Bible like the King James? Not on your life. His findings are very interesting to say the least. A job well done.

Before giving the last word, there needs to be a word or two said about lower case words for Deity. It seems that there are some people troubled by them when they read the Bible. But honestly it is not hard to figure out. They are used interchangeably at times, but mostly, just know that spelling was not standardized when the KJB came out in 1611. As such, it was not considered as being disrespectful.

It would be many years later before that would happen to the English language. For the readers information, attempts to update spelling, punctuation and paragraph markings took place in 1629, and 1638, both at Cambridge. Then Dr. F. S. Parris of the University of Cambridge in 1762, and R. Benjamin Blayney of the University of Oxford in 1769 both made changes in the KJB. The old Gothic or Germanic style of writing was changed to the Roman style, and attempts were made to standardize the text along with the correcting of several typographical errors due to printing errors. Finally, from 1866-1873, Dr. F. H. A. Scrivener completely standardized the text resulting in the 1873 Cambridge edition.

Please understand that the changes made to the

KJB were not revisions. Rather, they were standardizing the spelling and updating the punctuation, and paragraph marks. This information is important in light of the fact that the KJB critics take great delight and painstakingly try to prove that there were many revisions done to the Bible, but this does not square with the facts of history. So, do not let them to trip you up.

You might want to obtain a copy of Dr. David F. Reagan's booklet, *"The King James Version of 1611: The Myth of "Early Revisions"* to see for yourself the evidence.

Then, what about the word "thereof" in Scripture? Well now, there seems to be very many times this word appears in the word of God. This word is still in use today especially in legal documents. The term thereof is a combination of a demonstrative pronoun "there," and a preposition "of." It means of or of-it or of that or about the thought just mentioned. It is an adverb used when referring to an idea introduced earlier in the sentence. See Genesis 2:17, "thereof" or there of it. Meaning, Adam was not to eat of the "the tree of the knowledge of good and evil." If he did eat there in the Garden of Eden of it he would die that very day.

Let's take a look at 1 Timothy 6:10 which seems to trip some people up about the KJB. One of the peculiarities of the English Bible is 1 Timothy 6:10.

For the love of money is the root of all evil: which while some coveted after, they have erred from the faith, and pierced themselves through with many sorrows.

Reader, notice first what the verse does not say. 'The love of money WAS the root of all evil,' note the verb tense, IS. Further, the passage does not say, 'the love of money was the cause of all sin.' This is what all Bible corrupters think it says, but that is not correct. May I also add that it does not say that "money was the root of all evil." Again, reader, if you follow what the verse does not say, then you know that modern versions are wrong for what they say it means.

The verse does not need clarifying, altering, re-translated or even reworded. So, what exactly is this verse about, well, the love of money, greed, covetousness which is idolatry. See Eph. 5:4 and Col. 3:5; 1 Jn. 2:16; Gen. 3:6 and Exo. 20:17 all yield the correct meaning of 1 Timothy 6:10. Maybe you can take Exo. 20:3 along with the study. Oh, how about Eccl. 10:19? These should be enough to help anyone out.

British Spelling

Dear reader, if you're to better understand the word of God, one thing that is absolutely necessary to reading is to know that it is the ONLY English Bible on the market. That is, it was written in England, and therefore it has British spelling of words throughout both testaments. We will note only a few words to help you to see this truth contained in our KJB. One thing is sure, our Bible is written with proper grammar and is therefore foreign to most Americans. Sorry, but it had to be said at this point.

"Musick" or music Daniel 3:5. Incidently, all of Europe spells musick with a (k) on the end of the word, we of course do not, therefore Americans think it's misspelled. The same is true of the word "traffickers" in Isa. 23:8, remove the (k).

"Straightway" Mk. 5:42 for immediately, anon, still in use today in England. "Strait" is "narrow." Mt. 7:14

"Charity" 1 Thes. 3:6 is between believers only.

"Besought" Mk. 5:12 to entreat or implore.

"Devils" Mk. 5:15, demons. Many devils but one Satan and/or Devil, capitalized (Rev. 12:9.)

"Saith" Mk.5:19 is third person singular form of say, not said, for that is past tense form. It's present tense.

"Nigh" Mk. 5:21 for near or close by.

"Wept and wailed" Mk. 5:38 to weep, express sorrow audibly. Do you see why it's used?

"Damsel" Mk. 5:41 young unmarried woman of nobility.

"Prayed him" Mk. 5:18 for entreat or let one know.

"Stablished" Ps. 93:1 for place or set in

position.

"Established" Ps. 93:2 for to render stable or firm.

There are many other words which can be understood in their context such as: burnt for burned, whilst for while.

"Lighted off" Jos. 15:18 for landed or got off of.

Reader, look at how The New English Bible with Apocrypha handles the passage, "As she sat on the ass, she broke wind, and Caleb asked her, 'What did you mean by that?'" It is also in Judges 1:14 of the same book.

"Inasmuch" Mat. 25:40 is made up of three words, in as much, usually followed by as, means because, since, or according as.

"Insomuch" Mat. 8:24 made up of three words, in so much, usually has that with it, meaning seeing that, to such an extent.

"Conversation" Jas. 3:13; 1 Pet. 3:1 includes our behaviour.

"Iniquity" Attitude, intangible Ps. 64:6; 66:18; 28:3 No sacrifice for it, but, Isa. 53:5-6-Calvary.

"Transgression" a body breaks the laws-Rom. 4:15;

Jas. 2:11 "Sith thou hast" Context "Because", Ezekiel 35:6, 5, 10

Though there may be several other words having a British spelling, these will suffice for now and will help the reader somewhat. Some complain of words spelled two different ways, such as vail and veil, but they are the same. Take the word Louisville, it's pronounce two different ways but spelled the same way, and it's the same word though two different places (Louisville, KY and Louisville, MS).

Some words are spelled differently but pronounced the same way. As stated earlier, we all need to "study" the word of God (2 Tim. 2:15) for ourselves. It is this writer's hope that this book will help in that regard, and also other works used throughout this book.

Brings Understanding

The entrance of thy words giveth light; it giveth understanding unto the simple,

says Psalm 119:130.

In Psalm 119:104, we read,

Through thy precepts I get understanding: therefore I hate every false way.

Now, isn't that interesting? "Precepts" is another word for the Law of God, or the Bible in general. You see, saint of God, the Bible itself will give you understanding. Granted you have to be able to read it, but God grants the understanding. In previous verses in this 119th Psalm, verses 33, 66, 68 are just a few examples which tell us that it is God who teaches us His word. Please also note that even the Lord Jesus had to wait on His Father, who in turn gave Him understanding of His word.

In Psalms 119 again, consider this Messianic element in the following verses. In verses 98-100, we read,

> *Thou through thy commandments hast made me wiser than mine enemies: for they are ever with me. I have more understanding than all my teachers: for thy testimonies are my meditation. I understand more than the ancients, because I keep thy precepts.*

In Isaiah 50:4-5, it says,

> *The Lord GOD hath given me the tongue of the learned, that I should know how to speak a word in season to him that is weary: he wakeneth morning by morning, he wakeneth mine ear to hear as the learned. The Lord GOD hath opened mine ear, and I was not rebellious, neither turned away back.*

The Father teaches the Messiah, His Son, His word, and in so doing it made the Lord Jesus wiser than His enemies, for the Scriptures never left the Lord Jesus. As a result, Jesus also had more understanding than the teachers of His day. Jesus meditated on that word and obeyed the word of God and had more understanding than all of the elders of that day and time.

In Luke 2:40, 46-47 we read,

And the child grew, and waxed strong in spirit, filled with wisdom: and the grace of God was upon him. And it came to pass, that after three days they found him in the temple, sitting in the midst of the doctors, both hearing them, and asking them questions. And all that heard him were astonished at his understanding and answers.

But even so does God have to open up His word to us and as we meditate on it, it matures us in the faith. It can only do this for us because it is the perfectly preserved words of God according to passages like Ps. 12:6-7; Mtt. 24:35; 1 Pet. 2:2. But do not allow critics to throw you off course about those italicized words needed for clarity and correctness. For example, consider Deut. 8:3, where the term "word" is in italics, but Jesus quotes it in Mtt. 4:4 and it's not in italics. This proves that it should be in the text. Consider, "the brother of" in italics in 2 Sam. 21:19, but it is not in italics in 1 Chro. 20:5. For if it was not italics in 2 Samuel, there would be a lie in the word of God just as there is a lie in modern versions at this point. For another example of this see Acts 1:13 where we read the words "the brother" in italics but not in Jude 1. Just remember that it is all the words of God "from cover to cover." So, we read in Psalms 119:18,

Open thou mine eyes, that I may behold wondrous things out of thy law.

For further study consider the following passages: Ps. 1:2; Jn. 5:39; 2 Tim. 2:15; 1 Pet. 2:2.

Bibliography

Allen, Ward S., and Jacobs, Edwards C., The Coming of The King James Bible: A Collation of the Translators Work-in-Progress, The University of Arkansas Press, Fayetteville, 1995.

Bullinger, E. W., Figures of Speech Used In The Bible Explained And Illustrated, "Thomas Boys... (Commentary, 1 Pet. 3), London: New York; Eyre & Spottiswoode: E. & J. B. Young & Co., 1898, p.7.

Cloud, David, Way of Life Believer's Bible Dictionary, Bethel Baptist Print Ministry, Canada, 2015.

Daniel, David, The Bible In English: Its History and Influence, New Haven and London: Yale University Press, 2003.

Gipp, Samuel C., Ph.D., A Study of Verses Composed of Single Syllable Words, DayStar Publishing, Miamitown, Ohio, 2010.

Hills, Edward F., The King James Version Defended, The Christian Research Press, Des Moines, Iowa, 1956, 1984, 1988.

McClure, Alexander, Translators Revived, Mobile, AL, R. E. Publications, updated by R. E. Rhoades, 1858, 1974.

Moore, Hellen and Reid, Julian (eds.), Manifold Greatness: The Making of the King James Bible, Bodleian Library, University of Oxford, 2011, p. 102.

Nicholson, Adam, God's Secretaries: The Making of the King James Bible, Harper Perennial, 2003-2005.

Norton, David, A Textual History of the King James Bible, Cambridge University Press, 2005, p. 140.

Reagan, David F., The King James Version of 1611: The Myth of "Early Revisions", Antioch Publications Ministry, Knoxville, TN, 1986, 1996.

Riplinger, Gail, The Language of the King James Bible, A. V. Publications Corp., Ararat, VA, 1998.

Robertson, A.T., A Grammar of the Greek New Testament: In Light Of Historical Research, (Broadman Press, Nashville, 1934.)

Rosenau, William, Hebraisms In The Authorized Version, Reprint: Vance Publications, Pensacola, FL,1902,2002.

Ruckman, Peter S., Dr., Pastoral Epistles: I & II Timothy, And Titus, Bible Baptist Bookstore, Pensacola, FL,

Ryken, Leland, The Legacy of the King James Bible, Crossway, Wheaton, IL, 2011.

Still Waters Revival Books, The English Hexapla, Edmonton, AB, Canada, 1841.

Stringer, Phil, Biblical English, Faith Baptist Church Publications, Ft. Pierce, FL, 2000.

Vance, Laurence M., Archaic Words and the Authorized Version, Vance Publications, 1991.

Vance, Laurence W., The Angel of the Lord, Vance Publications, 1994.

Vance, Laurence W., King James, His Bible, And Its Translators, Vance Publications, 2006, 2016.

Waite, D. A., Dr., Defending the King James Bible: a Four-fold Superiority, Bible for Today Publications, Collingswood, N.J.

Webster, Noah, American Dictionary of The English Language, Foundation for American Christian Education, Chesapeake, VA, 1828, 1967, 1995, 2005.

Sightler, James H.,
www.sightlerpublications.com

Recommended Reference Guide

Hughes, Richard, An English Grammar for the

Study of Scripture, Richard Hughes Ministries, Inc., Cordele, GA, 2011. www.richardhughesministries.org

Scott, Paul W., English for Bible Readers, Morris Publishing, Kearney, NE, 2008.

SCRIPTURE REFERENCES

INDEX OF WORDS AND PHRASES

About the Author

Dr. Bobby J. Adams is an ordained Independent Baptist minister with over 40 years experience pastoring churches in MS, AR, and TN, and preaching in Bible conferences, revivals, and seminars. He has spoken on such subjects as the King James Bible and the Hebrew and Greek texts which underlie the KJB.

Dr. Adams received his A.A. from Clarke College, a B.A. degree with emphasis in New Testament Greek from Mississippi College University, his Th.M. and Th.D. from Andersonville Baptist Theological Seminary, and an honorary Ph.D. for co-authoring a book, editing a Greek grammar for a former Greek student, and work on an intermediary Greek reference guide.

Since those times, he has continued his studies to have a total of 21 hours in N.T. Greek, and 18 hours of Biblical Hebrew as well as teaching both these disciplines at Antioch Baptist College and Seminary. Currently, while pastoring Berea Baptist Church in Trenton, TN he heads up a Bible Institute under the authority of Berea Church.

Dr. Adams with his wife of 38 years, Lea, have

3 children and 5 grandchildren, and live in Rives, TN. This particular book came about trying to help God's people to get more into and out of the KJB.